# Contents

CW00340356

# Children of promise

Happy new year! Our readings in this issue lead us from God's perfect beginning in Genesis through the journeying of his people to the fulfilment of God's promises in Jesus, looking ahead to our glorious hope of resurrection in him.

The salvation promise is present throughout, from the hinted promise of Jesus in the Garden of Eden (Genesis 3:15), to the rainbow promise of Noah, and to Jesus himself. Difficult events pepper our Old Testament readings and challenge our thinking, yet, like Joshua, we are encouraged to be strong and not fear. And always in this quarter's readings, there are glimpses of Rahab's 'scarlet cord' (Joshua 2:15–18) reminding us of our salvation in Jesus and the faithfulness of our God.

Today, we and all other believers live in troubled times, in which the culture around us is at odds with God's intentions for his creation. The early Christians of Galatia and Corinth experienced it with pressures and disagreements from within; and from the adverse pressures of the surrounding culture. It can be difficult to say 'Yes' to God and 'No' to the world. Yet always,

as we're reminded through the words of Zephaniah, our God is watching over us.

Ultimately, our readings bring us to Jesus – 'the true and the new'. In him, in his death and resurrection, we find hope, renewal and the fulfilment of all God's promises. As we rejoice this coming Eastertide, as children of promise (Galatians 4:28), let's be still and listen to him: God's promises 'are "Yes" in Christ' (2 Corinthians 1:20).

**'Tricia and Emlyn Williams**
Editors

# Daily Bread toolbox

...icia & Emlyn
...lliams
...rked with
...ipture Union
...many years.
...lyn led Schools
...nistry, then
...rked with SU
...ernational.
...cia was also
...rt of the
...ools team and
...er worked for
...Publishing,
...veloping and
...ting Bible
...ources. In
...ent years,
...cia has been
...earching
...d writing
...out faith
...d dementia.
...v living in
...folk, they both
...tinue their
...ing, editing
...d talking-
...n-people
...istries, and
...involved in
...cal Anglican
...rch.

## WAY IN

This page introduces both the notes and the writer. It sets the scene and tells you what you need to know to get into each series.

## A DAY'S NOTE

The notes for each day include five key elements: *Prepare*, *Read* (the Bible passage for the day), *Explore*, *Respond* and *Bible in a year*. These are intended to provide a helpful way of meeting God in his Word.

## PREPARE

Prepare yourself to meet with God and pray that the Holy Spirit will help you to understand and respond to what you read.

## READ

Read the Bible passage, taking time to absorb and simply enjoy it. A verse or two from the Bible text is usually included on each page, but it's important to read the whole passage.

## EXPLORE

Explore the meaning of the passage, listening for what God may be saying to you. Before you read the comment, ask yourself: what is the main point of this passage? What is God showing me about himself or about my life? Is there a promise or a command, a warning or example to take special notice of?

## RESPOND

Respond in worship to what God has shown you in the passage, and pray for yourself and others. Decide how to share your discoveries with others.

## BIBLE IN A YEAR

If your aim is to know God and his Word more deeply, why not follow this plan and read the whole Bible in one year?

# Changed by faith

Through your support, SU trained church pastors Lox and Ruth Busisa* as Faith Guides so they could support young people without church backgrounds to explore the Bible and encounter and respond to Jesus. Being part of their group changed the life of teenager Ali** in ways she never would have dreamed possible.

*Pictured on page 6
**Pictured above left

Lox and Ruth lead LifePoint Church Pembrokeshire, located on a deprived estate in Haverfordwest. During the pandemic, SU helped them to connect with young people in the community through setting up regular sports ministry in the local park. On Sundays, they would have a short vibrant service, Church in the Park, open to all. 'That's when we first met Sammi and two of her children, Ali and Ethan,' says Lox. 'We got to know them and that autumn when we started a Friday group to connect with local teenagers Ali was among the ten young people who joined.'

**A life-changing adventure in Kenya**
Ali, then a shy girl in her early teens, had been going to a church youth group previously, but it had disbanded.

At Church in the Park, she heard how Lox and Ruth had founded their own charity in Kenya where Lox was from, and how they planned to take a group of teens from Haverfordwest to help work on projects there. 'Someone said that I should come too,' recalls Ali. 'But I'd never even left Pembrokeshire, I was terrified of flying and I had no idea how I would raise the £1,500 needed!'

Raising funds at a time when COVID restrictions really limited opportunities was indeed a challenge, but Ali rose to the occasion. 'I managed to get to £1,000,' she says, 'but two weeks before the deadline, I was still £500 short of my target. I prayed and the whole church prayed with and for me.

'A few days later someone made an anonymous donation to my bank of £500. I could go to Kenya and I was just so excited!

'Out in Kenya, our team helped build part of a disabled toilet and put filters into a water tank to give the village clean water. We distributed sports equipment to local people, and just helped out in the community however we could. It was amazing to see what Ruth and Lox do there, and to see God's help in that. And the worship at the churches was amazing!

'I knew about Christianity before, but it was only after going to Kenya and seeing and experiencing faith in action that I wanted to make a commitment and be baptised.'

**Many more prayers answered!**

Ali continued to experience God's presence on her return as she sat school exams. 'I get really stressed in exams but the church said they'd pray for me. In the exams I would pray for God's help, and the answers would just come to me. I passed all my exams, which I really didn't expect!'

Ali also used to get bullied at school which had robbed her of her self-confidence. Ali, together with Lox, Ruth and the rest of the church, prayed that she would get a Christian friend. 'Soon after,' says Ali, 'a girl called Tanatswa joined our year group in school. She was from Zimbabwe, and our teacher asked me to introduce her to other people and look after her. The first thing Tanatswa asked me was, "Are there any churches

# SU article

in Haverfordwest?" She was a Christian! So I brought her along to church, and she's been a really good friend to me.'

Tanatswa's welcome friendship was one of the many answers to prayer that God has given Ali.

### Fearfully and wonderfully made
Tanatswa and Ali both go to Lox and Ruth's Rooted youth group on a Wednesday evening. SU would term it as a Grow Community, meaning that most of the young people believe in Jesus but don't come from a church background as such. Ruth leads the group and says,

'The group are really open to exploring faith and ask lots of great questions. We have worship, Bible study and prayer, which our young people love – they are amazed they can speak to God and he hears! We use the SU Rooted journals to spark discussion and discover more about God and faith.'

Recently, Lox spoke to the group on Psalm 139. He says, 'I explained how the Bible says we are "fearfully and wonderfully made". At school, it's all about popularity – how many views you get on TikTok, how many likes you get on Instagram. But it's dependent on getting your clothes, make-up, hair, and so on right, in line with the latest trends which can change overnight. That constant need to compete and live up to some sort of unrealistic expectation messes them up.

'But I told them how God thinks they're awesome as they are. He doesn't look at their make-up, their hair, how they dress, their social media ratings. He sees through all those layers and loves them anyway, with a love that doesn't change.

'You could sense their relief. To know that God loves them, whatever their popularity rating, is something very unique and precious for them to be aware of and to hold on to, especially in these times of so much change.'

### 'Knowing God has changed me'
Ali agrees wholeheartedly. 'I used to wear lots of make-up and try and be who other people wanted me to be, rather than being myself.

'But knowing God has changed me. I'm learning to accept and to value the person he made me to be. My mum says I've blossomed. I've certainly grown in confidence. Even last year I would never have thought I could stand at the front of church and give a talk to lots of people – but now I can and I have! And I've helped run church events for over 60 children.'

When she turns 17, Ali hopes to go as a young leader on SLAM, a short, sports-based residential on the Gower which is organised by SU Mission Enabler Jack Newbould. Faith Guides bring groups of young people on it, and Ali was one of the teenagers that Lox and Ruth brought when it started in 2021.

Ali knows that God has a plan for her future, and it's a future that she's excited about! 'I used to dream of going to America and having my own YouTube channel and a big following, but God has given me a real change of heart. Now, more than anything, I want to study health and social care, and sociology, and become a mental health nurse.'

Please pray that God continues to guide and bless Ali, that she will grow in faith and knowledge of him, and in turn help inspire other young people to discover the God who loves them and accepts them – just as they are.

A shorter version of this story first appeared in *Connecting You*, Scripture Union's free quarterly supporter magazine. If you'd like to receive copies of *Connecting You* and learn more of how God is moving in the hearts and lives of children and young people today, you can sign up on our website at su.org.uk/connectingyou.

# East of Eden

**About the writer**
**Tanya Ferdinandusz**

Tanya and her husband Roshan have been married for 30 years and they have two adult sons – Daniel and Joshua. Tanya is both a freelance writer and freelance editor, and has been writing Bible reading notes, articles and devotionals for about 25 years. She is a Bible study leader and the author of *Marriage Matters*, a book for Christian couples.

'Go west' is not a compass direction but a reference to something going wrong or someone dying. In Genesis 1–11, however, it is going *eastward* that symbolises disaster! The garden God had 'planted ... in the east, in Eden' (2:8) was not just the setting for the creation story but the place where Adam and Eve enjoyed God's presence and blessings. After the fall, humanity's movement *away* from God is represented as going further east, *away* from the garden. Adam and Eve were banished and sent *eastward* – with God's angel-guard on the 'east side' (3:24); driven from God's presence, Cain settled in 'Nod, east of Eden' (4:16); and the Babel-builders not only 'moved eastward' but settled in Shinar (11:1,2), which is Babylon – the city that epitomised rebellion against God.

The beginning of another year is a great time to revisit Genesis 1–11, which records many beginnings: the universe, life, work, marriage; the beginning of things so 'good' going so wrong; but also the beginning of God's redemptive work: a seed-promise (3:15), a covenant (9:8–17), and then the stage being set for God's grand redemption story, as Abram's family leave Ur in the east to head westward towards Canaan (11:31; 12:1–5).

Reflect on how the characters in Genesis 1–11 either draw nearer to God or move further away from him. Consider your own life direction: How will you move forward in a godly and God-ward direction in 2024?

# How great thou art!

## PREPARE

'O Lord, my God, when I in awesome wonder, consider all the works thy hands have made...'* Prayerfully consider what God has made and done in your life.

## READ

**Genesis 1:1 – 2:3**

## EXPLORE

Genesis 1 is not, and was never intended to be, a scientific explanation of how the world was created, but a revelation and declaration of how great God is. These verses are not scientific statements but a story – not a fanciful fairy tale, but foundational truths encapsulated in story form. This carefully crafted creation story takes us where science does not and cannot go, exploring not merely what God has done, but who God is and who we are in relation to him.

More than 30 references to God, what God said and did (making, naming, blessing) and his view of creation ('God saw that it was good') underscore some fundamental truths. First, creation is God's. As its owner-ruler, God appointed his image-bearers as representative rulers and trustees of his creation (1:26–28). While free to use and enjoy the earth and its resources, God holds us accountable for our stewardship of this sacred trust. Secondly, as the designer-developer of human life, God alone knows how life and relationships work best; and so the wise will live according to the Maker's manual. Thirdly, creation is good; matter is neither evil nor unspiritual, and how we manage the material world, including our bodies, matters to God (see 1 Timothy 4:1–5).

God blessed them and said ... 'Rule over the fish in the sea and the birds in the sky and over every living creature that moves on the ground.'

**Genesis 1:28**

## RESPOND

Let your prayerful reflection on the creation story move your heart to exclaim, 'How good, how gracious, how great thou art!'

*'How Great Thou Art', see http://CMMS/hymnSong.php?id=pd00016ehymnbook.org/

**Bible in a year:** Genesis 1,2; Acts 1

# Boundary-ed blessings

## PREPARE

'... love the LORD your God ... walk in obedience to him ... keep his commands, decrees and laws; then ... the LORD your God will bless you' (Deuteronomy 30:16). Think about how keeping God's 'laws' yields rich blessings in different areas of life.

## READ

Genesis 2:4–25

## EXPLORE

Life was good in Eden. God himself had planted the garden, provided a river to water it, and 'made all kinds of trees grow' for utility – 'good for food' – and beauty – 'pleasing to the eye' (vs 8–10). Adam and Eve enjoyed fruitful and fulfilling work (v 15), the blessed companionship of a harmonious partnership (vs 18–25) and a share in the abundant life of God himself through unrestricted access to the 'tree of life' (v 9). They had everything they needed, not simply to survive but to thrive.

But God's boundless blessings are boundary-ed! Just as God has established boundaries in nature – for example, setting limits on the sea, which symbolised the forces of chaos (Genesis 1:9,10) – he also sets boundaries for his people (vs 16,17). Satan would have us believe that boundary-less living is an attractive alternative (Genesis 3:4,5). But without boundaries, there is no protective framework to keep out fear, shame and guilt, and to create a safe space within which we may freely explore, experience and enjoy God's blessings. By breaking bounds, we place ourselves outside this place of blessing (Genesis 3:23); and there, stripped of divine protection, fruitfulness and flourishing are replaced by futility and frustration.

> ... 'You are free to eat from any tree in the garden; but you must not eat from the tree of the knowledge of good and evil ...'
>
> **Genesis 2:16,17**

## RESPOND

Do you need to rethink your attitude to God's boundaries?

# Anatomy of temptation

## PREPARE
'I've banked your promises in the vault of my heart so I won't sin myself bankrupt' (Psalm 119:11, *The Message*). Memorise a promise to 'bank' in your heart!

## READ
**Genesis 3:1–13**

## EXPLORE
Medical students diligently study anatomy. Understanding the human body helps them to diagnose what has gone wrong with their patients. Christians must be diligent students of the anatomy of temptation! Dissecting Satan's subtle strategies enables us to recognise temptation's pull.

Satan distorts God's Word. Asking 'Did God really say…?' (v 1) plants a niggling seed of doubt in Eve's mind and 'smuggles in the assumption that God's word is subject to our judgment'.* The permission to eat from 'any tree' except one (Genesis 2:16,17) is turned on its head, casting doubt on God's character, portraying him as tight-fisted and restrictive rather than benevolent and wise. Consider whether a narrow focus on prohibitions sometimes causes you to lose sight of God's wide-ranging permissions and his forest of blessings…

Satan also dismisses God's warning. 'You will not certainly die' (v 4) makes God out to be a liar. The devil then deceives Eve with an empty promise: 'You will be like God' (v 5). The creation story repeatedly affirms, 'God saw that it was good' (Genesis 1:4,10,12,18,21,25,31). But Eve made her choice based on what *she* 'saw' was 'good' (v 6), ignoring God's command and usurping the divine prerogative to determine good and evil (v 5).

> … 'Did God really say, "You must not eat from any tree in the garden"?'
> **Genesis 3:1**

## RESPOND
Eve's story is an example to avoid. Jesus gives us an example to emulate. Contrast how the anatomy of temptation plays out in Matthew 4:1–11.

*Derek Kidner, *Genesis*, IVP, 2005, p67

**Bible in a year:** Genesis 5,6; Acts 3

# Harmony to hostility

## PREPARE
Reflect: 'Every action that we take exacts a cost and produces consequences. Nothing can be undone.'*

## READ
**Genesis 3:14–24**

## EXPLORE
Sin's entrance wrecked the order characterising Genesis 1 and 2, setting in motion a principle of brokenness that would for ever affect every person and every part of creation. Cracks would emerge in three key areas. First, instead of unbroken fellowship with God, humanity would be embroiled in a painful battle with evil (v 15). Secondly, harmony between men and women would turn to hostility (v 16). Thirdly, the earth would be resistant to human toil, only reluctantly fruitful, while 'groaning' under the burden of humanity's exploitation (vs 17–19; Romans 8:20–22).

Although often viewed as the story's 'punishment' element – an angry judge pronouncing sentence on wrongdoers – there is another way to interpret today's passage. When we disregard the manufacturer's instructions for using an appliance, it may break, malfunction or cause injury. Similarly, deviating from

God's design has adverse consequences for his creation. God's pronouncements (vs 16–19) need not be interpreted as punishments imposed but, rather, as predictions about how the inevitable consequences of sin would play out over time. In relation to marriage, for example, 'Genesis 3:16 is not God's prescription for a new order, but description of the disorder that reigns when sin is allowed the upper hand. God isn't pronouncing a punishment; he's simply predicting that a hostile power struggle will undermine a once harmonious partnership.'**

> '... he will crush your head, and you will strike his heel.'
>
> **Genesis 3:15**

## RESPOND
Place your hope in Jesus, who 'entered the disordered mess of struggling humanity in order to set it right ...' (Romans 8:3, *The Message*).

*Kilroy J Oldster, *Dead Toad Scrolls*, Booklocker.com Inc, 2015
**Tanya Ferdinandusz, *Marriage Matters*, Back to the Bible, 2018, p129

**Bible in a year:** Genesis 7,8;  Psalms 1,2

# Sin-ripples

## PREPARE

Pray for God's grace to 'be alert and of sober mind' because 'the devil prowls around like a roaring lion looking for someone to devour' (1 Peter 5:8).

## READ

**Genesis 4:1–26**

## EXPLORE

How does a worshipper, entering God's presence with an offering (v 3), end up a 'restless wanderer', cut off from God's presence (vs 14,16)?

Cain was 'very angry' that his offering was rejected (v 5). Yet, God did not punish Cain but, with the probing question, 'Why are you angry?' (v 6), invited Cain to search his heart and get right with God (see Genesis 3:9,11,13 for more such questions). Cain ignored both the question and God's wise counsel to 'do what is right' (v 7). His unrepentant anger made him easily led to commit murder.

'Sins are like circles in the water when a stone is thrown into it; one produces another. When anger was in Cain's heart, murder was not far off.'* As Jesus taught, anger leads to further sin and makes us as culpable as if we committed murder (Matthew 5:22).

Genesis 3 and 4 show humankind becoming increasingly hardened to sin: 'Eve had to be talked into her sin; Cain could not be talked out of it, even by God himself.'** Lamech went still further – he could not *stop* talking about his sin (vs 23,24)!

> '... if you do not do what is right, sin is crouching at your door; it desires to have you, but you must rule over it.'
>
> **Genesis 4:7**

## RESPOND

'The journey from your mind to your hands is shorter than you're thinking.'*** Are you harbouring in your mind or heart something that must be nipped in the bud before it reaches your hands?

*Matthew Henry, cited in John Bate, *Six Thousand Illustrations of Moral and Religious Truths*, 1899, p798
**Steven J Cole, https://bible.org/seriespage/lesson-11-sin-crouching-door-genesis-41-15, 1996
***Mark Hall, 'Slow Fade', My Refuge Music and Sony/ATV Tree Publishing, © 2007

**Bible in a year:** Genesis 9–11; Acts 4

Genesis 5:1–32

# In the midst of life...

## PREPARE
Reflect: 'In the midst of life we are in death.'*

## READ
**Genesis 5:1–32**

## EXPLORE
How is today's chapter – a long list of names of long-ago people who lived very long lives! – relevant to modern people?

The re-statement of the truth that the human race was created in God's image (vs 1,2) emphasises that everyone in 'Adam's family line' – like Adam himself – is created in God's likeness. Despite sin's entrance (Genesis 3) and its escalation (Genesis 4), we continue to bear God's image. Adam's family line continues to multiply (all these people 'had other sons and daughters'), showing that God's creation blessing of fruitfulness had not been withdrawn. Nevertheless, all these accounts (except two) conclude by noting, 'and then he died' – a sobering reminder that in the midst of life, death inevitably intervenes, interrupting the blessing of life. Even Methuselah, who could undoubtedly make it into the *Guinness* (or Genesis!) *Book of World Records*, ultimately died at the ripe old age of 969 years.

Two people stand out. Enoch was spared death and mysteriously whisked away by God (vs 21–24; Hebrews 11:5). Noah, although he would ultimately die, was spared death in the great flood and used by God to give humanity a fresh start. Both Enoch and Noah 'walked faithfully with God' (vs 22,24; Genesis 6:9), a phrase that echoes the pre-fall intimacy Adam and Eve enjoyed with God (Genesis 3:8). Despite human sinfulness, blessed fellowship with God remains a glorious possibility for all of us.

## When God created mankind, he made them in the likeness of God.
**Genesis 5:1**

## RESPOND
Pray: 'Teach us to number our days, that we may gain a heart of wisdom' (Psalm 90:12).

*'The Order for the Burial of the Dead: At the Grave', The Book of Common Prayer, 1928

**Bible in a year:** Genesis 12,13;  Acts 5

# Trust amid tension

## PREPARE
Draw strength from Jesus' promise: 'I have told you these things, so that in me you may have peace. In this world you will have trouble. But take heart! I have overcome the world' (John 16:33).

. . . . . . . . . . . . . . . . . . . . . . . . . . . . . . . . . . . . . . . . . . . . . . . . . . . . . . . . . . . . . . . . . . . . .

## READ
Psalm 120

## EXPLORE
In lamenting that he must 'dwell in Meshek' and 'live among' the people of 'Kedar' (v 5) – both far from the Promised Land – the psalmist is not giving us a precise location pin! Rather, he is expressing the troublesome tensions of being compelled to live away from his true home, among people who do not share his worldview: although he is committed to 'peace', they 'hate peace' and supported 'war' (vs 6,7).

Christians are 'still in the world' though 'not of the world' (John 17:11,14), and 'God's election to membership in his family set[s] them in a paradoxical situation – non-members in a world in which they must continue to live.'* The resulting tension not only produces a sense of alienation, it often provokes hostility – like the slander the psalmist faced (vs 1,2). Jesus declared, 'Blessed are the peacemakers' (Matthew 5:9). But peacemakers do not always feel very 'blessed'; sometimes, they feel more like crying, 'Woe to me' (v 5)! Nevertheless, despite his present 'distress' (vs 1,2), the psalmist remains confident of God's ultimate deliverance (vs 3,4) and committed to 'speak' out 'for peace' (v 7).

I am for peace; but when I speak, they are for war.
Psalm 120:7

## RESPOND
Tomorrow, we will read about Noah, whose righteousness set him apart from the people of his time (Genesis 6:9). Amid trials and tensions, are you consciously and conscientiously striving to stand for righteousness and speak out for peace?

*Ralph P Martin and Peter H Davids (eds), *Dictionary of the Later New Testament and its Developments*, IVP, 2000

. . . . . . . . . . . . . . . . . . . . . . . . . . . . . . . . . . . . . . . . . . . . . . . . . . . . . . . . . . . . . . . . . . . . .

**Bible in a year:** Genesis 14,15;  Psalms 3,4

# A factory reset

## PREPARE
'Sin is not just breaking God's laws; it is breaking his heart' (Adrian Rogers).

## READ
**Genesis 6:1–22**

## EXPLORE
When my phone stopped working, I was distraught. The restart option failed. Powering off and on again did not resolve the problem. A factory reset was the only solution. In the process, I lost precious data – contacts, chats and photos.

God's creation was not working according to his design. Sin had increased exponentially: 'every inclination of the thoughts of the human heart was only evil all the time' (v 5). The meaning of the reference to 'sons of God' marrying 'daughters of humans' (v 2) is unclear but, like Lamech's polygamy (Genesis 4:19), was probably another, more serious, distortion of God's design for marriage. In the beginning, God 'saw' that creation was 'good' (Genesis 1); all he 'saw' now was 'how great the wickedness of the human race had become' (v 5).

God had tried both persuasion and punishment (see Genesis 3:8–13; 4:6–12), to no avail. Even drastically reducing human lifespans (v 3) had not succeeded in halting the spread of corruption and violence (vs 11,12). Finally, God decreed a factory reset. In the process, many lives were lost and the earth itself was destroyed by the great flood. While God's intention was to 'destroy' (vs 13,17), he did not choose this course of action lightly: 'his heart was deeply troubled' (v 6). It was grief, not rage, that gripped God, an attitude mirrored in Jesus as he wept over the judgement that would befall Jerusalem (Luke 19:41–44).

> The LORD regretted that he had made human beings ... and his heart was deeply troubled.
>
> **Genesis 6:6**

## RESPOND
'Don't grieve God. Don't break his heart' (Ephesians 4:30, *The Message*). Reflect on this today.

**Bible in a year:** Genesis 16,17; Acts 6

# A righteous remnant

## PREPARE

'Things fall apart; the centre cannot hold; / Mere anarchy is loosed upon the world.'* These words were penned in the aftermath of the First World War. Reflect on their relevance for today.

## READ

Genesis 7:1–24

## EXPLORE

Genesis 3 portrays judgement as the outworking of the consequences of sinful choices (see 4 January). In Genesis 7, judgement is effected by the removal of God's restraints. At creation, God brought order out of disorder by separating the waters above from the waters below (Genesis 1:6,7). In the flood, God removed these restraints; and as 'the springs of the great deep burst forth, and the floodgates of the heavens were opened' (v 11), the earth returned to a state resembling original chaos (vs 17–23; compare Genesis 1:2). Yet, despite the heavy loss of life, all was not lost; and there is repeated emphasis on the measures God took to ensure the survival of the species (vs 1–3,7–9,13–16).

A 'remnant' has been described as 'what is left of a community after it undergoes a catastrophe'.** Noah represents the faithful 'remnant' – a recurring term in scripture. Despite the wickedness of the human race (Genesis 6:5), God used a righteous man called Noah (v 1) to preserve a remnant of his people who would survive the flood and be the means of a fresh start for humanity.

The LORD then said to Noah, 'Go into the ark, you and your whole family, because I have found you righteous in this generation.'

**Genesis 7:1**

## RESPOND

'So too, at the present time there is a remnant chosen by grace' (Romans 11:5). Are you among those chosen by grace?

---

*WB Yeats, 'The Second Coming', https://www.poetryfoundation.org/poems/43290/the-second-coming
**Anchor Bible Dictionary, Volume V, Yale University Press, 2007, p669

**Bible in a year:** Genesis 18,19; Acts 7

## Wednesday 10 January
Genesis 8:1–22

# A God who remembers

## PREPARE
Contemplate God's promise: 'I will not forget you! See, I have engraved you on the palms of my hands' (Isaiah 49:15,16).

## READ
**Genesis 8:1–22**

## EXPLORE
It rained relentlessly for 40 days and 'the waters flooded the earth' for 150 days (Genesis 7:12,24). Noah had been shut inside that ark for over 6 months! However, the comment 'but God remembered Noah' (v 1) does not imply that Noah's plight had previously slipped God's memory. God never forgets his people or his promises. But 'God's remembering always implies his movement towards the object of his memory'.* To say God remembers is to say that he acts, either in mercy or in judgement, to fulfil his promises.

God's remembering 'combines the ideas of faithful love … and timely intervention'.** When God remembered Noah, he intervened by sending 'a wind' that made the flood waters recede (v 1). This 'wind' recalls both the Spirit, who hovered over the watery chaos at creation (Genesis 1:2), and 'the strong east wind' that drove back the Red Sea in Israel's great redemption story (Exodus 14:21).

Genesis 6–9 has a mirror-image (chiastic) structure, with Genesis 8:1 as the central verse that divides the text into two parallel sections. The first section describes a 'de-creation' – the unravelling of God's creation work (6:9 – 7:24). God's remembrance of Noah is the pivotal turning point where God begins to reverse the effects of the flood in a work of 're-creation' (8:2 – 9:28).***

> But God remembered Noah … and he sent a wind over the earth, and the waters receded.
>
> **Genesis 8:1**

## RESPOND
How will you remember and respond to the Lord who remembers you and will keep his every promise?

*BS Childs, *Memory and Tradition in Israel*, SCM, 1962, p34
**Derek Kidner, *Genesis*, IVP, 2005, p92
***See Gordon J Wenham, J Alec Motyer, DA Carson and RT France (eds), *New Bible Commentary*, IVP, 1994

**Bible in a year:** Genesis 20,21; Acts 8

# Take two

## PREPARE

'Whoever oppresses the poor shows contempt for their Maker, but whoever is kind to the needy honours God' (Proverbs 14:31). How can you show kindness to those in need?

## READ

**Genesis 9:1–29**

## EXPLORE

After the 'factory reset' of Genesis 6 (see 8 January), humanity received a fresh start. Although God's opening words to Noah (v 1) closely resemble the creation mandate of Genesis 1:28, 'Take two' is not quite the way we used to be – not because of any flaws in God's original design but due to humanity's fallen nature. God's mandate factors in human sinfulness: while humankind will continue to exercise dominion over the rest of creation, their rule is now marked by 'fear and dread' (v 2), and their 'fellow-creatures' will be their food* (v 3). No wonder there is hostility between humans and other creatures.

In the sphere of human relationships, God anticipated that hostility would even escalate to murder. So, right at the outset, before binding himself in a unilateral covenant with all creation (vs 9–17), God affirms two truths: first, all human life is valuable, simply by virtue of being created as God's image-bearers (v 6b); and secondly, every human being will be held accountable for how they treat those who bear God's image (vs 5,6).

'Take two' does not get off to a promising start! Before the chapter is over, Noah is found drunk, and Ham dishonours his father (vs 20–25).

'Whoever sheds human blood, by humans shall their blood be shed; for in the image of God has God made mankind.'

**Genesis 9:6**

## RESPOND

In *Animal Farm*, the pigs change the 'All animals are equal' rule by adding, 'but some animals are more equal than others'!** How do we – as nations, communities, or individuals – sometimes do the same?

*Derek Kidner, *Genesis*, IVP, 2005, p100
**George Orwell, *Animal Farm*, Harcourt, Brace & World, 1946, p148

**Bible in a year:** Genesis 22,23; Psalms 5,6

**Friday 12 January**
Genesis 10:1–32

# Table of nations

## PREPARE
Reflect on the hymn lyric: 'Thou dost all nations rule, / And their affairs control; / Thy power extends o'er all the earth, / Thy love from pole to pole' (Anon).

## READ
Genesis 10:1–32

## EXPLORE
Genesis 1–11 takes a wide-angle view of humanity, repeatedly emphasising that all people are God's image-bearers, created and blessed by God (1:26–28; 5:1,2; 9:6,7). After the flood, God bound himself by a covenant with Noah and his 'descendants' for 'all generations to come' (9:8–12). It is these 'descendants' of Noah who are named in Genesis 10 – nations or their founders, including some familiar names: Babylon, Assyria, Egypt, Canaan, Sodom and Gomorrah (vs 10,11,13,15,19).

In Genesis 12, the camera zooms in on Abraham, Israel's founding father, who comes from the line of Shem (10:31; 11:10–26). Although in most of the Old Testament the camera remains trained on Israel, God's choice of this *one* nation never excludes other nations, even though these nations frequently opposed both God and Israel. God's promise to Abraham was not just to make Israel 'a great nation'; rather, his purpose is as wide as the world: 'all peoples on earth will be blessed through you' (Genesis 12:2,3).

Genesis 10 – sometimes called the 'Table of Nations' – lists 70 nations, and Jesus' sending out of the 70 (or 72) probably symbolised the good news going to all nations (Luke 10:1). As Christ-followers, we are also commissioned by Jesus to 'make disciples of all nations' (Matthew 28:19).

> These are the clans of Noah's sons, according to their lines of descent, within their nations. From these the nations spread out over the earth ...
>
> **Genesis 10:32**

## RESPOND
Make this your prayer for our world: 'Let Your glory fall in this room / Let it go forth from here to the nations.'*

*David Ruis, Mercy/Vineyard Publishing (ASCAP), © 1992

**Bible in a year:** Genesis 24,25; Acts 9

# How the mighty have fallen

## PREPARE

'The kings of the earth rise up and the rulers band together against the Lord ... saying, "Let us break their chains and throw off their shackles"' (Psalm 2:2,3). How might these words be relevant in our own times?

- - - - - - - - - - - - - - - - - - - - - - - - - - - - - - - - - - - - - - - - - - - - - - - - - - - - -

## READ

**Genesis 11:1–32**

## EXPLORE

God's mandate to 'rule over' creation included the command to 'fill the earth' (Genesis 1:28). This necessitated spreading out, not settling down. The Babel builders defied this decree when they settled down at Shinar (v 2). Their 'Project Babel' envisioned a mega-city, whose mission statement read: 'make a name for ourselves' (v 4)! Puffed up with pride, greedy for glory, their desire for a tower that reached the heavens echoes that earliest temptation to 'be like God' (Genesis 3:5).

Sometimes, 'united we stand' is neither good nor true! These people united against God in an act of fruitless rebellion: 'Why do the nations conspire and the peoples plot in vain?' (Psalm 2:1). Ironically, God had to 'come down' just to 'see' this great city and tower (v 5)! Their arrogant attempts to exalt themselves resulted in their being brought low and put in their place – literally, put in different *places* as they dispersed across the earth, as God had originally decreed. Just as the flood resulted in chaos, the builders are left 'confused' (v 9). Another 'fall' marks another low point in human history. But God's grace will reach down yet again, this time through the line of Shem, to raise up Abram, Israel's founding father (vs 10–32).

'... let us build ourselves a city, with a tower that reaches to the heavens, so that we may make a name for ourselves ...'
**Genesis 11:4**

### RESPOND

Whose kingdom are you building? Whose purposes are you serving?

- - - - - - - - - - - - - - - - - - - - - - - - - - - - - - - - - - - - - - - - - - - - - - - - - - - - -

**Bible in a year:** Genesis 26,27; Acts 10

# The mountain-maker

## PREPARE
'Some trust in chariots and some in horses, but we trust in the name of the LORD'
(Psalm 20:7).

## READ
Psalm 121

## EXPLORE
Picture the psalmist, climbing slowly up Temple Mount, on pilgrimage to God's house. As he lifted his eyes to the distant mountains, did he fear the robbers' haunts on the hillsides? Was he thinking of some secret refuge up in the mountains (see Psalm 11:1)? Or was he contemplating his destination – that magnificent Temple? No matter what 'the mountains' represent, the psalmist's central message is clear: a believer's security does not lie in created things – like mountains – but in the mountain-maker, 'the Maker of heaven and earth' (vs 1,2).

The repeated phrase 'watch(es) over' (vs 3–5,7,8) is a guarantee of comprehensive coverage. The pilgrim is promised protection against all kinds of threats – accidents (v 3a), the elements (vs 5,6) and other perils (vs 7); he is assured of protection at all times – for God is never off duty (vs 3,4) – and for all times ('now and for evermore', v 8b); and this protection covers all situations ('your coming and going', v 8a). God's CCTV cameras scan in all directions and he monitors them 24/7! But the protection gets even more personal: 'The LORD watches over you' (v 5). Throughout our faith journey, the mountain-maker himself is our bodyguard and soul-guard, sticking close, guarding and guiding us safely to our destination – himself.

> My help comes from the LORD, the Maker of heaven and earth.
>
> **Psalm 121:2**

## RESPOND
Pray: 'God of peace, walk through this week with me. Like a sentinel, let your peace stand guard over my heart and mind, shielding me from faithless fears and fruitless worries.'*

*Based on Philippians 4:7,9

**Bible in a year:** Genesis 28,29; Psalms 7,8

# REVEALING
# JESUS

**FREE:**
COACHING
AMAZING RESOURCES
ADVICE & SUPPORT

## A flexible and FREE mission framework from Scripture Union

Helping you journey into faith with children and young people who aren't in church.

· · · · · · · · · · · ·

SU.ORG.UK/REVEALINGJESUS

# Kiss the world beautiful

The writing of this series commenced in Milton Keynes and was completed in Lahore, during two weeks in which I joined my wife visiting her parents in her native Pakistan. During that time, I made my home in a culture vastly different from my own. On an entirely different scale, these readings bring the bold declaration of John that, in Jesus, God 'made his dwelling among us' (1:14); that he came from eternity to earth to 'pitch his tent' within his creation.

John's Gospel is therefore an up-close and personal account of the life of God on earth – of what happened when ordinary women and men encountered God in the flesh during their everyday lives. This being so, there is always a danger that in writing on John's Gospel 'the Word made flesh here is made word again', to quote from a poem by Edwin Muir* in which he takes preachers to task for confining the mystery of the incarnation of Christ in lifeless, ideological words.

Aware of this potential pitfall, the notes that follow are offered in the prayerful hope of helping readers encounter the living Christ – the Word made flesh – through the opening chapters of John's account of Jesus. John's stated purpose in writing his Gospel is that readers 'may believe that Jesus is the Messiah, the Son of God' (20:31). This series, therefore, has that same purpose.

## About the writer
### Nigel Hopper

An accredited Baptist minister, and former Managing Editor for Scripture Union's Bible resources, Nigel now works for the John Lewis Partnership. He is married to Nudrat, and lives in Milton Keynes.

*Edwin Muir, 'The Incarnate One', in *One Foot in Eden*, Faber & Faber, 1956

# One of us

## PREPARE

God is with you in this moment; take time to delight in his presence now.

## READ

**John 1:1–18**

## EXPLORE

Having just completed a two-week series in the opening chapters of Genesis, you may have had a sense of déjà vu as you read the first verses of John's Gospel. Commencing his account of the life of Jesus with the words, 'In the beginning was the Word...' (v 1), John echoes the 'In the beginning God...' of Genesis 1:1. The echo is deliberate and serves to frame John's story of Jesus as the story of God's new creation. All that follows should be viewed through the lens of the God of all wisdom, who spoke creation into being, being present on earth in Jesus to bring about the renewal of that creation!

Often referred to as the 'prologue' to John's Gospel, these verses summarise the main thrust of his message and introduce key themes that are woven throughout the rest of the book. Not least among these is the theme of light and darkness (vs 4–5,7–9), a literary device that speaks powerfully of the conflict that characterises so much of Jesus' earthly ministry. As children of God through faith in Christ (v 12), to what extent should Christians expect to similarly encounter adversity as well as adventure in the way of discipleship?

The Word became flesh and made his dwelling among us.

**John 1:14**

## RESPOND

Thank God for the signs you see of his new creation breaking in on the world; bring before him any fears you have about situations where you fear the light of Christ is not welcome.

**Bible in a year:** Genesis 30,31;  Acts 11

# He never said

## PREPARE

'He guides the humble in what is right and teaches them his way' (Psalm 25:9). If possible, kneel before God in humility now.

## READ

**John 1:19–28**

## EXPLORE

When you really want a particular job, you encounter the temptation to claim more about yourself than you properly should. The need to 'sell yourself' to a prospective employer can lead to some very creative expressions of professional and personal achievements!

John the Baptist must have been similarly tempted when it came to responding to the questions of the priests and Levites (v 19), and Pharisees (v 24), regarding his status. Since they're asking, why not suggest, at least, that he might indeed be Elijah, or a prophet (v 21), or even the Messiah (v 20)? John, however, resists the temptation, identifying himself emphatically as only the 'support act' to the 'headlining' Christ to follow (vs 23,26,27).

The spiritual insight and humility of John is contrasted with the spiritual ignorance and pride of the religious leaders who question him and who, by virtue of their office, really should have perceived that God was at work in his activities. They are in the dark when it comes to the light about which John testifies (v 19). God is not constrained by our proudly held prescriptions for how he must work, and through whom he will work.

> He did not fail to confess, but confessed freely, 'I am not the Messiah.'
>
> **John 1:20**

## RESPOND

Confess before God your own prejudices about what his activity looks like. Ask him to open your heart and mind to his infinite possibilities.

**Bible in a year:** Genesis 32,33; Acts 12

# This light is ours

## PREPARE

Think of your favourite title for Jesus. Talk to God about the reasons for your choice and give him thanks for the gift of his Son.

..................................................................................................

## READ

**John 1:29-34**

## EXPLORE

Boxer Muhammad Ali was the 'Greatest'; singer Elvis Presley, the 'King of Rock and Roll'; and former UK Prime Minister Margaret Thatcher, the 'Iron Lady'. These are all examples of famous epithets – titles given to people to convey their character and/or significance. The epithet bestowed on Jesus by John the Baptist here is the 'Lamb of God' (v 29). We have no idea what John's contemporaries would have made of this designation, but within the narrative of the Gospel it looks ahead at the outset to the climactic, sacrificial death of Jesus as God's Passover lamb (19:28–37). John is consistent in wanting nothing more than to make Jesus known.

It is significant that John amplifies his epithet: Jesus is 'the Lamb of God, who takes away the sin of the world!' (v 29). With this we are informed that the scope of the new creation that God will work in Jesus is truly cosmic. Through him, all people everywhere – not just Israelites – can receive the Holy Spirit (v 33) and become children of God (1:12,13). Jesus, the Messiah (v 34), is the 'light for the Gentiles' (Isaiah 49:6). To what extent does this make God the God of equality, diversity and inclusion?

> The next day John saw Jesus coming towards him and said, 'Look, the Lamb of God, who takes away the sin of the world!'
>
> **John 1:29**

## RESPOND

Ask God to help you see those whom you secretly regard as beyond his salvation as being as much a focus of his work of new creation as yourself.

..................................................................................................

**Bible in a year:** Genesis 34–36; Acts 13

# I will follow

## PREPARE
Thank God for those people who played a part in introducing Jesus to you.

. . . . . . . . . . . . . . . . . . . . . . . . . . . . . . . . . . . . . . . . . . . . . . . . . . . . . . . . . . . . . . . . . . . .

## READ
**John 1:35–42**

## EXPLORE
Imagine being greeted at church by someone pointing to another church down the road and suggesting you go there if you're serious about getting on board with what God is doing! That's essentially the challenge with which John the Baptist confronts two of his own disciples here. Consistently identifying Jesus as greater than himself (v 36), John positively wants his followers to transfer their allegiance to Jesus, which they do (v 37). It's a refreshingly selfless approach that reveals John to be concerned only with God's extension of his kingdom through Christ, and not with building his own empire. To what extent can the same be said of us and our churches?

What is also refreshing in these verses (and John's Gospel as a whole) is the absence of any programmatic recruitment strategy on Jesus' part. Instead, potential followers are simply introduced to him, both conversationally and personally, by those already 'in the know' about him (vs 36,37,41,42). It's worth a thought, isn't it?

Following Jesus means, first and foremost, being with him (v 39). However, Jesus' renaming of Simon as Peter (v 42) reminds us that those whom Jesus accepts as they are do not remain as they are; they find themselves caught up in God's work of new creation.

## 'We have found the Messiah' (that is, the Christ).
**John 1:41**

## RESPOND
What might God need you to do to ensure his work of new creation is not hindered by a focus on church rather than kingdom in your context?

. . . . . . . . . . . . . . . . . . . . . . . . . . . . . . . . . . . . . . . . . . . . . . . . . . . . . . . . . . . . . . . . . . . .

**Bible in a year:** Genesis 37,38; Psalm 9

# Change your world

## PREPARE
Ask God to open your heart and mind to receive his Word now.

## READ
**John 1:43–51**

## EXPLORE

One of the charges politicians delight to level against each other when a proposed course of action is suddenly abandoned is that of performing a policy U-turn. Opponents seize on this as evidence of political weakness and/or incompetence. Sometimes, however, a U-turn is the right and necessary response to compelling new insight.

Nathanael is presented here as a man well versed in the Scriptures. Seen as places of security and peace (eg Micah 4:4, Zechariah 3:10), rabbinic writing suggests it was common for Jewish men to sit under the shade of fig trees (v 48) for their scriptural meditation and debates. Philip's words (v 45) pick up on Nathanael's thinking (v 46). His conviction that Israel's Messiah could not possibly come from Nazareth (v 46) is founded on his reading of the Law. That reading must be radically revised, however, when he encounters Jesus, who reads him incisively and who knows his position (vs 47,48). Nathanael's U-turn is confirmed with his declaration that Jesus is indeed the 'king of Israel' (v 49).

It is to Nathanael's credit that he revises his reading of the written word in response to his encounter with the Word made flesh. His example reminds us that we should come to the Bible with humility, asking not so much, 'What do I make of this word?' but rather, 'What does the living Word revealed here make of me?'

> Then Nathanael declared, 'Rabbi, you are the Son of God; you are the king of Israel.'
> **John 1:49**

## RESPOND
Meditate on what God wants to make of you through your reading of his Word today.

**Bible in a year:** Genesis 39,40; Acts 14

# Every little sign

## PREPARE
Reflect on the transformation Jesus has brought to your life; give thanks and praise to God.

## READ
John 2:1–12

## EXPLORE
In John's Gospel, Jesus' miracles are always 'signs' (v 11). That means they point beyond themselves to the central truth that Jesus is the Messiah (20:30,31), and that in him God is at work to bring about the renewal of his creation (1:1). Jesus' changing of water into wine at the wedding feast in Cana (vs 8,9) is therefore more than an act of compassion to save a family's blushes. It is indicative of the transformation God is bringing to his creation through Jesus, and therefore of the honour due to Jesus as the Messiah.

That honour is expressed as obedience by the servants at the feast who, as Mary instructs them (v 5), do whatever Jesus tells them (vs 7,8). The blessing of the new wine flows from humble obedience to Jesus. The detail that the jars filled with water were those used by Jews for ceremonial washing (v 6) is significant. That washing was a sign pointing to the purification that would ultimately come through Jesus' sacrificial death – his 'hour' (v 4). The transformation of the water in the jars into wine therefore 'calls time' on the need for ceremonial washing. Now that Jesus the Messiah is dwelling among his people, it is to him and not to established rituals that they must hold.

> His mother said to the servants, 'Do whatever he tells you.'
>
> **John 2:5**

## RESPOND
In what do you find obedience to Jesus most difficult? Ask for grace to do whatever he tells you in this matter.

**Bible in a year:** Genesis 41,42;  Acts 15

# Going home

## PREPARE
Think of all that you love about the place where you live, and praise God for his blessings.

## READ
Psalm 122

## EXPLORE

This psalm is one that Israelite pilgrims would have sung as they made their way to Jerusalem to celebrate one of the great Jewish festivals (v 4). It is a joyful celebration of the city and all that it stands for, both religiously and politically (vs 1–5). Religiously, Jerusalem is home to the Temple – symbol of God's presence with his people (v 1). Politically, Jerusalem is the seat of God's justice – both social and economic – for his people (v 5). Then, as now, what happens in the city shapes the lives, hopes and well-being of those who live beyond the city, and God is interested in every sphere of life.

This song is also a summons to pray for the peace and prosperity of Jerusalem (vs 6–9). The prayer is that the city should be a focus of peace (vs 6–8) – a centre for the flourishing of all creation, living in the presence of God and under his reign. Christians believe that

Jesus is the fulfilment of Jerusalem's religious and political functions. This psalm therefore confronts us with the challenge not only to pray for the peace of Jerusalem and other cities, but also to play our part as children of God in making our cities centres for the flourishing and well-being of all creation.

For the sake of my family and friends, I will say, 'Peace be within you.'
Psalm 122:8

## RESPOND
Pray for the city, town or village in which you live, that it may be a centre for justice and the flourishing of all God's creation.

**Bible in a year:** Genesis 43,44; Psalm 10

# Strange way

## PREPARE
Ask God to remove anything that might distract your focus as you prepare to encounter him through his Word now.

## READ
**John 2:13–25**

## EXPLORE

An old proverb states that 'a new broom sweeps clean', meaning that those newly appointed to positions of authority often make sweeping changes to reinvigorate an organisation. Jesus' 'sweeping clean' of the Jerusalem Temple (vs 15,16) goes much further. He isn't interested in reinvigorating the Temple; he is demonstrating that he replaces the Temple! The dramatic public disturbance declares that the Temple will soon be obsolete.

The clue to this interpretation of events is Jesus' likening of his own body to a temple (vs 19–21), which is effectively a claim that he – and no longer the Temple building – is now the focal point of God's presence on earth. The old Temple and its feasts, including Passover (v 13), pointed to Jesus and his sacrificial death as the Lamb of God – his being consumed by zeal for the family ('house') of God (v 17). With the Word now made flesh, Temple worship and ritual, like ceremonial washing, must give way to worship of Jesus the Messiah.

The anger of Jesus towards the Temple traders suggests that the intended symbolic significance of the Temple and its offerings had long since been sacrificed to concern for commercial interests. When our own religious rituals cease to be at heart about our relationship with God through Christ, they too cease to be relevant.

His disciples remembered that it is written: 'Zeal for your house will consume me.'

**John 2:17**

## RESPOND
What lessons, if any, can churches learn from Jesus' clearing of the Temple regarding their involvement in commercial enterprise?

**Bible in a year:** Genesis 45,46; Acts 16

# The fading of light

## PREPARE
Pray for wisdom to understand what God wants to say to you through his Word today.

........................................................

## READ
John 3:1–21

## EXPLORE
It's tempting to think sometimes that if we could just find the right way to present the message of the gospel then people would understand the attraction of Jesus and make the decision to follow him. This passage tells us otherwise. Here, Nicodemus is granted a one-to-one audience with Jesus himself who explains that a person 'must be born again' (v 7), but Nicodemus just doesn't understand (v 10). Israel's teacher (v 10) comes to Jesus at night (v 2) and remains firmly in the dark about God's unfolding new creation in Christ.

Do you think that Nicodemus simply can't understand Jesus' teaching, or that he refuses to do so? Jesus' insistence that entry into God's kingdom is dependent not on physical birth into Judaism, but on responding in faith to him as Messiah at the prompting of the Spirit (vs 3–8,13–18), would certainly have posed a major challenge to Nicodemus' thinking

as a leading figure in the religious establishment (v 1). Rather than judge Nicodemus, however, we would do better to reflect long and hard on the extent to which our own purported concern to guard Christian truth is actually a self-serving – and ultimately futile – attempt to contain and control the wind of the Spirit that 'blows wherever it pleases' (v 8).

For God so loved the world that he gave his one and only Son, that whoever believes in him shall not perish but have eternal life.

**John 3:16**

## RESPOND
What might be the implications of this passage for both personal and church approaches to evangelism?

**Bible in a year:** Genesis 47,48; Acts 17

# Love the light in you

## PREPARE
Spend a few moments meditating on the words of Philippians 2:5–8.

· · · · · · · · · · · · · · · · · · · · · · · · · · · · · · · · · · · · · · · · · · · · · · · · · · · · · · · · · · · · · · · ·

## READ
### John 3:22–36

## EXPLORE
In unprecedented scenes, supporters of Donald Trump stormed the US Capitol building on 6 January 2021. Refusing to accept that he had lost the 2020 presidential election to Joe Biden, Trump's supporters were attempting to block the official certification of the results. Power can so easily exert an illegitimate hold even on those who have held it legitimately. In contrast, John the Baptist demonstrates a refreshingly different relationship to power in these verses.

Confronted by his disciples, who were jealous of the growing Jesus movement and concerned for the implied decline in the popularity of their own movement (v 26), John responds with an expression of delight that Jesus is in the ascendancy (vs 29,30). Whereas his disciples view the growing popularity of Jesus as a loss to lament, John himself sees it as a joy to behold. Even though

he has tasted a degree of power and popularity himself, John recognises that Israel – the bride – belongs not to him, but to Jesus – the Messiah (vs 28,29).

John knows not only who Jesus is (vs 31–36), but also who he is in relation to Jesus (vs 27,28). It is in this knowledge that John's remarkable humility is rooted, which in turn gives rise to his complete contentment with doing no more than God's will – even when that requires his fading from prominence (v 30).

> 'He must become greater; I must become less.'
>
> **John 3:30**

## RESPOND
Consider whether there is any situation in which God's unfolding new creation requires you to become less. Take action accordingly.

· · · · · · · · · · · · · · · · · · · · · · · · · · · · · · · · · · · · · · · · · · · · · · · · · · · · · · · · · · · · · · · ·

**Bible in a year:** Genesis 49,50; Acts 18

# Please, sir

## PREPARE
Pray for your Christian sisters and brothers around the world, thanking God for them and the diversity within the family of faith.

## READ
**John 4:1–26**

## EXPLORE
This interaction between Jesus and the Samaritan woman bears the hallmarks of a courtship ritual. It is reminiscent of the first meeting between Jacob and Rachel, who later became his wife (Genesis 29:1–30). It is therefore appropriate to see Jesus – just identified by John the Baptist as the bridegroom (3:29) – as leading the Samaritan woman on, not towards marriage but revelation!

In its cultural context, the identification of the woman as both a woman and a Samaritan (v 7) and her arrival at the well in the middle of the day (v 6) to avoid the disapproval of the townsfolk who knew her reputation (vs 17,18), all emphasise the gulf between her and Jesus, and therefore the inappropriateness of their encounter. Jesus, however, subverts all these societal stereotypes by willingly engaging the woman in conversation (v 7). Imagine the impact on her self-esteem! How often might the simple choice to talk to someone enable us to see them in God's light?

Like Nicodemus (3:1–21), the Samaritan woman is given one-to-one teaching from Jesus (vs 10,13,14,21–24). Unlike Nicodemus (see also John 19:38–42), however, she receives Jesus' teaching and is rewarded with the revelation that he is the Messiah (v 26) – the person who as the focus of worship makes the place of worship irrelevant (vs 21–24).

> The Samaritan woman said to him, 'You are a Jew and I am a Samaritan woman. How can you ask me for a drink?'
>
> **John 4:9**

## RESPOND
Who does God want you to talk to by way of demonstrating his love for them? Start the conversation today.

**Bible in a year:** Exodus 1,2; Psalms 11,12

# Down to the well

## PREPARE
Ask God to reinvigorate your faith as you encounter him through his Word today.

● ● ● ● ● ● ● ● ● ● ● ● ● ● ● ● ● ● ● ● ● ● ● ● ● ● ● ● ● ● ● ● ● ● ● ● ● ● ● ● ● ● ● ●

## READ
**John 4:27–42**

## EXPLORE
This passage is brimming with excitement. So excited is the Samaritan woman following her encounter with Jesus that she returns to share openly with the very townsfolk she had previously wanted to avoid how Jesus knew all about her sex life (vs 28,29)! Jesus himself is excited by his exchange with the Samaritan woman, telling his disciples of how the realisation that she and her community were ready to receive the gospel energised him as food nourishes the body (vs 32–38). The Samaritan woman's townsfolk are excited not only by what she has to say (v 39), but also by the teaching they receive first-hand from Jesus himself (vs 40–42). This is what happens when God's new creation unfolds in the person and through the work of Jesus – lives are transformed.

After two days in his company (v 40), the Samaritans declare Jesus to be the 'Saviour of the world' (v 42). The scope of God's new creation extends beyond ethnic boundaries to embrace all creation! 'Saviour of the world' was a title the occupying Roman Emperors took to themselves – so to ascribe it to Jesus was to make a political statement, thereby emphasising that the transformation of a new creation is public as well as private. If we refrain from political engagement, we deny the extent of God's redemptive purposes.

'Come, see a man who told me everything I've ever done. Could this be the Messiah?'

**John 4:29**

## RESPOND
How can Christians and churches effectively demonstrate the transformative impact of God's new creation in public and political life?

● ● ● ● ● ● ● ● ● ● ● ● ● ● ● ● ● ● ● ● ● ● ● ● ● ● ● ● ● ● ● ● ● ● ● ● ● ● ● ● ● ● ● ●

**Bible in a year:** Exodus 3,4;  Acts 19

# Just like the man said

## PREPARE
'Sovereign LORD, you are God! Your covenant is trustworthy...' (2 Samuel 7:28). Meditate on this truth with thankfulness.

## READ
**John 4:43–54**

## EXPLORE
Imagine visiting a landmark tourist attraction only to realise on your departure that you'd spent so long viewing the visitor information boards that you never focused on the landmark itself! The importance of avoiding that danger in relation to Jesus is in view here.

The healing of the royal official's son is designated a sign by John (v 54), but one the official doesn't need to see to believe. Although initially assuming Jesus' physical presence would be required (vs 47,49), the official is content to take Jesus at his word (v 50). He believes that the Word who spoke creation into being (1:3) can speak new creation into being in the life of his son. The detail about the precise timing of the healing (vs 52,53) emphasises the appropriateness of his faith.

Jesus can be taken at his word and requires faith without the need of signs as proof (v 48). Our faith should not be in the flesh but in the Word made flesh (1:14): in other words, faith in the Messiah himself and not in the marks of the Messiah. To allow the latter to distract from the former is to mould Jesus in our image rather than allowing him to renew the image of God in us.

> The man took Jesus at his word and departed.
>
> **John 4:50**

## RESPOND
Listen now for whatever word God has for you. Resolve to take him at his word when it becomes clear to you.

**Bible in a year:** Exodus 5,6; Acts 20

# No peace

## PREPARE
Recall a time when you experienced God's presence in a time of trouble. Rejoice in his love and faithfulness.

## READ
**Psalm 123**

## EXPLORE
There are times in life when we've had enough and need something to change for the better. At such times, it's tempting to take matters into our own hands, but this psalm reminds us that it is into God's hands that we should place our predicament.

Psalm 123 is the song of God's people who have had enough of the contempt of the wealthy and arrogant who exploit them (v 4). This is, in a sense, a protest song – one that God's people would sing en route to Jerusalem where they would seek justice. It is trusting dependence on God – like that of an employee assured that their employer will act in their best interests – that gives voice to this song (v 2). God's people can ask for his mercy, assured that he desires to show mercy (vs 2,3).

The honesty of expression in this song reveals it to be a prayer of hope of those who know what it is for their prayers not to be answered instantly – the singers have already endured 'no end of contempt' (vs 3,4). This psalm is therefore a gift to all God's people today who, wherever they are in the world, must cling to the hope of his mercy amid adversity.

Have mercy on us, LORD, have mercy on us, for we have endured no end of contempt.

**Psalm 123:3**

## RESPOND
Use the words of this psalm to talk honestly with God about your need of his mercy, and to express your expectant hope of his renewing intervention.

**Bible in a year:** Exodus 7,8; Psalms 13,14

# The scarlet cord

## About the writer
**Tony Horsfall**

Tony is an author, retreat leader and mentor based in Bournemouth. He is married to Jilly, and attends GodFirst Church in Christchurch.

The book of Joshua tells how the people of Israel eventually entered the Promised Land after leaving Egypt and wandering in the wilderness for 40 years. Moses was dead, and Joshua had succeeded him as leader. The whole generation of those who left Egypt had died in the wilderness (excluding Joshua and Caleb), so it was a new generation that crossed the Jordan.

The story centres on Joshua and describes how he grew into leadership and how God used him to inspire Israel into taking the land. Yet the victory was not Joshua's but God's. Throughout the book we see that this was the Lord's doing. The land was his gift to his people, their inheritance which they did not earn. In this we are taught that God is the great Giver, and we receive from his grace. He initiates and directs; we respond with faith and obedience. This is the way of victory and how the Christian life is to be lived.

This does not mean we are passive, however. Joshua has to show great courage, and the people have to learn to obey. Above all they must consecrate themselves to God, separating themselves from sin and being devoted to doing God's will.

Joshua is an inspiring read, yet it presents a challenge to modern readers, especially in the level of violence. If we see beyond this, it will strengthen our faith and deepen our commitment to God.

## Monday 29 January
Joshua 1:1–9

# A hard act to follow

### PREPARE
Ask God to speak to you as we begin these readings in Joshua, especially that you will have the courage to rise to the challenge of following Jesus in today's world.

### READ
**Joshua 1:1–9**

### EXPLORE
It has been said that success without a successor is failure, but leadership transitions can be tricky. Joshua is called by God to take over from Moses. What big shoes he has to fill! I wonder if he feels daunted by the task.

God speaks to reassure his servant and reminds him of two important resources to help him meet the challenge. First, his presence will be with Joshua (v 5). When God calls us, he promises to accompany us and to equip us for the task. He will be alongside us in every situation we face, leading and directing us, strengthening and upholding us.

Secondly, God's Word (the Book of the Law) will be Joshua's guide (v 8). We are also to meditate on scripture, absorb its wisdom then live it out. That way we will be successful.

God will bring his people into the land he has promised them. It is primarily his

work. At the same time, Joshua must find within himself the strength of mind and depth of character to persevere. He must be resilient and brave, strong and courageous. There will be big challenges ahead (v 9).

> 'As I was with Moses, so I will be with you; I will never leave you nor forsake you. Be strong and courageous.'
> **Joshua 1:5,6**

### RESPOND
What challenges are you facing at home, in work or at church? How can God's presence strengthen you? How is God speaking to you through his Word, so you become more confident and less fearful?

---

**Bible in a year:** Exodus 9,10; Acts 21

# People get ready

## PREPARE

Before starting the day, we take time to get ourselves ready. Coming before God requires heart preparation. Take time to be still, breathe slowly and be mindful that you are drawing near to God.

## READ

**Joshua 1:10–18**

## EXPLORE

A major emphasis in the book of Joshua is that God is giving them the land, just as he promised to Abraham and the other patriarchs so long ago. They will inherit the land as a gift, but at the same time must go and take possession of it. Here is an abiding principle: God initiates and we respond; God gives, and we receive.

Although the Reubenites, Gadites and the half-tribe of Manasseh have permission to stay on the eastern side of the Jordan, they must still be involved in capturing the land and be ready to fight alongside the other tribes (vs 12–15). Their response is commendable for they do not wish to shirk their responsibilities (vs 16–18).

Notice too how they encourage Joshua, promising the same allegiance to him they gave to Moses, encouraging him with a timely reminder that God will be with him, exhorting him to be strong and brave (v 18). All leaders, however confident they may appear, need the support of those they lead. Don't assume because they appear competent and in control that leaders do not wrestle with insecurity and the need for affirmation.

> 'Get your provisions ready. Three days from now you will cross the Jordan here to go in and take possession of the land the LORD your God is giving you.'
>
> **Joshua 1:11**

## RESPOND

Are you ever tempted to shirk responsibilities, opting for a comfortable life? How can you show support to your leaders? What words of encouragement might God ask you to share today?

**Bible in a year:** Exodus 11,12; Acts 22

## Wednesday 31 January
Joshua 2:1–16

# An unlikely ally

## PREPARE
It is easy to misjudge people. Ask that God will give you his love today for everyone you meet, regardless of their appearance or background.

. . . . . . . . . . . . . . . . . . . . . . . . . . . . . . . . . . . . . . . . . . . . . . . . . . . . . . . . . . . . . . . . . . . .

## READ
Joshua 2:1–16

## EXPLORE
Rahab is a surprising person to find listed among the heroes of faith, but there she is alongside Abraham and other notable people (Hebrews 11:31). By welcoming the spies, and hiding them, she showed herself to be on God's side.

Rahab is also commended by James for demonstrating her faith through her actions (James 2:25,26). Despite her background, she finds her way into the genealogy of Jesus (Matthew 1:5).

Like us, Rahab was not perfect, but she clearly believes and acts out her conviction. She has heard the stories of Israel's crossing of the Red Sea and defeat of neighbouring kings. She knows that 'the LORD your God is God in heaven above and on earth below' (v 11). Her life oozes with kindness and courage, and she plays an essential part in the conquest of the Promised Land.

Rahab's story reminds us not to judge people too quickly or harshly. God's allies can be found in some unlikely places. All of us are in process, and none of us is the finished article.

'I know that the LORD has given this land to you … and that a great fear of you has fallen on us, so that all who live in this country are melting in fear because of you.'

**Joshua 2:9**

## RESPOND
How is your faith being expressed in your life? In particular, how are you demonstrating kindness to those you meet? How do you respond to those who have faith and yet are clearly still in the process of transformation?

. . . . . . . . . . . . . . . . . . . . . . . . . . . . . . . . . . . . . . . . . . . . . . . . . . . . . . . . . . . . . . . . . . . .

**Bible in a year:** Exodus 13,14;  Acts 23

# The scarlet cord

## PREPARE

Pray today that God will give you ears to hear his Word, and that you will also have the grace to respond in obedience. Come before God with an openness to receive his Word.

• • • • • • • • • • • • • • • • • • • • • • • • • • • • • • • • • • • • • • • • • • • • • • • • • • • • •

## READ

**Joshua 2:17–24**

## EXPLORE

The scarlet cord appears to be a sign of good faith between Rahab and the spies. Both parties need assurance that the other can be trusted. Is it reading too much into the text to suggest that the colour scarlet is a reminder of the blood painted over doorposts during the Exodus (Exodus 12:7,13), and therefore that it points us to the blood of Jesus?

By tying the cord to her window, Rahab expresses her allegiance to the God of Israel, a risky thing to do because she might appear as a traitor, yet she is desperate for her family to be saved as well as herself (2:13). Their safety lies in looking to God for protection. She must trust that the men will keep their promise.

The spies for their part commit themselves on oath to be as good as their word, and to deal kindly and faithfully with Rahab and her family when, in God's timing, Jericho is captured (v 14). Integrity and reliability are good characteristics that reflect the nature of God. How we deal with others is an important part of our testimony.

> So she sent them away, and they departed. And she tied the scarlet cord in the window.
>
> **Joshua 2:21**

## RESPOND

What promises or assurances have you made to other people? Have you kept your word? If not, how can you make amends? Why does it matter? If you have been let down by someone, how might you respond?

• • • • • • • • • • • • • • • • • • • • • • • • • • • • • • • • • • • • • • • • • • • • • • • • • • • • •

**Bible in a year:** Exodus 15,16;  Psalm 15

# Crossing the Jordan

## PREPARE
Jesus asked Bartimaeus, the blind man, 'What do you want me to do for you?' (Mark 10:51). Ponder that question as you come to God. How will you answer?

## READ
**Joshua 3:1–17**

## EXPLORE
After many years of wandering in the wilderness, and centuries since the promises were first given to Abraham, the people of Israel are about to enter the Promised Land. First, however, they must cross the Jordan, a serious obstacle since it was in flood (v 15) and the people were many.

Consecration is the act of setting oneself apart to God for a particular purpose. It involves getting our hearts right before him and choosing again to do his will. Such heart preparation is often the prelude to a new movement of God in our lives. Joshua calls the people to prepare themselves to enter the land by offering themselves afresh to God (v 5).

The ark symbolised the presence of God. Although other nations may have regarded it as some kind of talisman, to Israel it was as if God himself went before them. It gave them confidence.

As the priests enter the waters of the Jordan, a miracle happens: the waters part and the people cross over on dry ground (vs 16,17), just as in the crossing of the Red Sea (Exodus 14:21,22). It is God's doing.

Joshua told the people, 'Consecrate yourselves, for tomorrow the LORD will do amazing things among you.'
**Joshua 3:5**

## RESPOND
Do you long to see God at work in and through your life? The key is to surrender yourself to him so he can use you for his glory. Take time to yield every part of your life to him.

**Bible in a year:** Exodus 17,18; Acts 24

# What do the stones mean?

## PREPARE

Take a moment to think of any highlights on your spiritual journey. Review some of your memorable experiences and give thanks to God for positive memories of people, places and events.

## READ

**Joshua 4:1-9**

## EXPLORE

Crossing the Jordan must have been a memorable experience for all involved, and a vivid lesson in the power of God. If God could stop the Jordan in full flow, then he could certainly give them the land.

Yet how easily we forget such lessons with the passing of time. Joshua is told to choose 12 men, one for each tribe, and tell each man to take a sizeable stone from the middle of the Jordan, carry it over to the other side and set it down with the others where they have camped (vs 2,3). This pile of stones is to be a memorial, reminding them how God turned back the waters so they could cross over (vs 6,7). It will speak of his power and faithfulness.

The message of the stones need not be lost, for in the future children will ask about their meaning. The stones will become a great object lesson for future generations about the greatness of God. They will help parents teach their children and grandchildren what it means to believe in God. This transmission of faith, based on personal testimony, is a natural way to teach others about God.

'Each of you is to take up a stone on his shoulder, according to the number of the tribes of the Israelites, to serve as a sign among you.'

**Joshua 4:5,6**

## RESPOND

What stories can you share about the love and power of God? How can you pass on your faith to other generations?

**Bible in a year:** Exodus 19,20; Acts 25

## Sunday 4 February
Psalm 124

# If God is for us...

## PREPARE
Are you able to make space for God today in a more leisurely way than normal? Take time to be still and quiet – and thank God for the gift of rest.

## READ
**Psalm 124**

## EXPLORE
This battle psalm sits well in the context of a series on the book of Joshua. It was written by David, probably during his skirmishes with the Philistines (eg 2 Samuel 5:17–25).

The message is clear: without God's help Israel would have been overwhelmed, but he came to their aid and gave them victory. As Paul reminds us in Romans 8:31: 'If God is for us, who can be against us?' We too may feel overwhelmed, but we can count on the same divine intervention.

Many graphic images are used to describe Israel's plight: being eaten alive (v 3), swept away in a flood (v 4) or ripped to pieces (v 6). The one that stands out to me, though, is that of a tiny, defenceless bird that has been snared and captured, only to be set free to fly again (v 7). This beautiful image of freedom from captivity speaks to us of

the way God liberates us from bondage to sin and enslavement to addictions. God is on the side of all who desire a better life and to be free from life-destroying habits. No matter what our circumstances, God is our helper. He is on our side.

Our help is in the name of the LORD, the Maker of heaven and earth.
**Psalm 124:8**

## RESPOND
Do you feel overwhelmed? Trapped and helpless, like that little bird? Remember God is your helper and your deliverer. He is able to save you, and to set you free.

**Bible in a year:** Exodus 21,22; Psalm 16

# Ready for battle

## PREPARE
Remind yourself today that Jesus not only died but rose again. He has defeated sin, Satan and death and now reigns victorious in heaven. And we reign with him.

## READ
**Joshua 4:10 – 5:1**

## EXPLORE
We may not like to think of the Christian life as a battle, but it is. Our struggle is not against people, as Paul reminds us, but against principalities and powers, demonic forces who represent the kingdom of Satan (Ephesians 6:12).

Crossing the Jordan, although miraculous, was in some ways the easy part. Capturing the land would be much harder and would not happen without a fight. The Canaanite tribes would not surrender their land meekly but would contest the advance of Israel. That is why, when Israel crosses over, they are 'ready for battle' with about 40,000 men prepared for war (4:12,13). We are reminded of Paul's vivid description of the armour of God that we are to wear as we face our own spiritual foes (Ephesians 6:13–17) and his call to face suffering 'like a good soldier of Christ Jesus' (2 Timothy 2:3).

Recent events have validated Joshua's leadership credentials and established him as commander of the armies of Israel. In this he is like Jesus, the exalted head of the church and our victorious leader.

> That day the LORD exalted Joshua in the sight of all Israel; and they stood in awe of him all the days of his life, just as they had stood in awe of Moses.
>
> **Joshua 4:14**

## RESPOND
In what ways are you aware of the spiritual battle? Where do you see Satan's activity in the world, and how does he come against you? Take time to put on the armour of God today so you can stand against his wiles.

**Bible in a year:** Exodus 23,24; Acts 26

## Tuesday 6 February
Joshua 5:2–12

# Painful surrender

### PREPARE
Forgiveness is a wonderful gift from God. When we confess our sins, he not only forgives us but lifts the shame from us. Ponder this amazing truth as you draw near to God.

### READ
**Joshua 5:2–12**

### EXPLORE
Circumcision was a sign of the covenant between God and Israel, but a whole generation of men had grown up in the desert without it (vs 5–7). Now Joshua is told to circumcise all those men of military age to remind them they are God's covenant people, set apart and different from the surrounding peoples.

Strategically it seems a strange thing to do just before a period of warfare, for the men would be incapacitated and need time to heal, making them vulnerable to attack (v 8). However, this is not a normal sort of warfare. With God, obedience matters most of all.

Physical circumcision represents a deeper spiritual work of God, the cutting away of rebellion and disobedience, and the surrender of the heart to God (Romans 2:28,29). Indeed, the apostle Paul says that the truly circumcised are those who 'serve God by his Spirit, who boast in Christ Jesus, and who put no confidence in the flesh' (Philippians 3:3).

This surrender paved the way for the celebration of Passover, and the end of eating only manna. Egypt was behind them and a whole new, abundant life ahead (vs 11,12).

> Then the LORD said to Joshua, 'Today I have rolled away the reproach of Egypt from you.'
> **Joshua 5:9**

### RESPOND
When we surrender to God, we surrender not to force but to love. Take time to offer yourself to God, allowing him 'cut away' anything unhelpful in your life.

**Bible in a year:** Exodus 25,26; Acts 27

# The fall of Jericho

## PREPARE

Bring to God today any problematic situation that looms large before you and seems to be without solution. The God who caused Jericho to fall is your God. He is able!

## READ

**Joshua 5:13 – 6:20**

## EXPLORE

The conquest of Jericho begins with Joshua's encounter with a mysterious armed stranger who turns out to be commander of the army of the Lord (5:13–15). This heavenly figure is probably the angel of the Lord (a term that can mean either a messenger of God or possibly God himself in the Old Testament), or even, as some suggest, a pre-incarnate appearance of Jesus. Either way, it is a moment for Joshua to surrender himself to God before the battle and recognise that Israel is not fighting for God: God is fighting for them.

This is an amazing story of the power of God to demolish strongholds and deal with impossibilities. It is all God's doing, and victory is given, not gained. Yet it requires faith on the part of Israel to follow the rather unorthodox battle plan that is given to Joshua. It must have required great self-control to march around the city so many times

in silence, apart from the trumpets blowing (vs 6–11). Once again, the ark symbolises the presence of God, the key ingredient in the heavenly strategy. Finally, on the last time around as they give a battle cry, the walls come tumbling down, a pure act of God (6:20).

Then the LORD said to Joshua, 'See, I have delivered Jericho into your hands, along with its king and its fighting men.'

**Joshua 6:2**

## RESPOND

The way through difficult circumstances often begins with yielding to God, and asking that his will be done. Remember that the battle belongs to the Lord. Lay your burdens in faith at his feet. Nothing is too difficult for him.

**Bible in a year:** Exodus 27,28; Acts 28

## Thursday 8 February
Joshua 6:21-27

# Judgement and salvation

## PREPARE
Today's passage is a difficult one. Pray that God will give you his perspective and a humility to trust him for what you may not understand.

## READ
Joshua 6:21-27

## EXPLORE
The wholesale destruction of Jericho is hard to accept. Old Testament scholar Chris Wright says, 'There is something about this part of the Bible that I have to include in my basket of things I don't understand about God and his ways.'* Can we make any sense of such violence?

The Canaanite tribes were guilty, like Sodom and Gomorrah, of extreme human wickedness (Leviticus 18:24,25). For this reason, God drove them out of the land to cleanse and purge it. Like a surgeon removing cancer, radical surgery was required to prevent further spread of the disease. It was an act of justice which their wickedness deserved. The destruction of Jericho would act as a deterrent to other cities, minimising resistance and reducing further casualties. Justice always carries an element of deterrent.

At the same time the mercy of God is seen in that Rahab (a future ancestor of Jesus) and her circle are spared the destruction (vs 17,25). The implication is that others who turned to the God of Israel would also be spared. There is no clear-cut solution to the problem, however. We must trust that God's ways are right, even when they are beyond our understanding.

> But Joshua spared Rahab the prostitute, with her family ... because she hid the men Joshua had sent as spies to Jericho – and she lives among the Israelites to this day.
>
> **Joshua 6:25**

## RESPOND
If you struggle with passages like this, why not talk to someone well-versed in the Old Testament? Or search the internet for books and articles?

*Chris Wright, *The God I Don't Understand*, Zondervan, 2008, p86

**Bible in a year:** Exodus 29,30; Psalm 17

# Joshua's parting words

## PREPARE
Gratitude is a spiritual discipline. We *choose* to remember what God has done. Take time today to reflect on the good things God has done for you and given to you.

. . . . . . . . . . . . . . . . . . . . . . . . . . . . . . . . . . . . . . . . . . . . . . . . . . . . . . . . . . . . . . .

## READ
**Joshua 23:1–16**

## EXPLORE
I am often introduced these days as an 'elder statesman', a designation I quite enjoy! Like Joshua, I am not afraid to acknowledge my age, although I baulk at saying I am *very* old. With age comes perspective, and hopefully a little wisdom. From his position of 'having seen it all', Joshua exhorts the people of Israel with some fatherly advice, encouraging them to be mindful of God's goodness to them in the past as they move into the future:

Be grateful (v 3). They have taken possession of the land only because God has worked on their behalf. God has given them victory.

Be obedient (v 6). They are to follow the example of Joshua, being careful to obey God's Word. This is the pathway to blessing.

Be steadfast (v 8). God has been faithful to them, so they are to be loyal to him, refusing to turn away to other gods.

Be loving (v 11). God has loved them, and they are to love him in return. This is a relationship of love, not law.

Joshua's advice has timeless relevance. Here is a pattern for Christian living that is worth following.

> 'You know with all your heart and soul that not one of all the good promises the LORD your God gave you has failed. Every promise has been fulfilled; not one has failed.'
> **Joshua 23:14**

## RESPOND
For what are you grateful? In what way is God asking you to be obedient? What does it mean for you to hold fast? How are you expressing your love for God?

. . . . . . . . . . . . . . . . . . . . . . . . . . . . . . . . . . . . . . . . . . . . . . . . . . . . . . . . . . . . . . .

**Bible in a year:** Exodus 31,32;  Matthew 1

# We will serve the Lord

## PREPARE
Following Jesus is a choice. When did the journey begin for you? Review your spiritual history and pray that you will have grace to keep following wherever he leads you.

## READ
**Joshua 24:1–31**

## EXPLORE
Joshua gives the people a history lesson. From the very moment of Abraham's call, God had been faithful to his people, leading and guiding them, and doing for them what they could never do themselves. Their history was a story of grace, of God at work on their behalf. Everything they now possess has been given by God. All is attributable to his grace. How then should they live?

For Joshua this a moment of decision. He is clear that he and his family will continue to serve the Lord, but what of Israel? He puts them on the spot and makes them decide who they will follow (v 15). Three times they affirm their decision:

We will serve the Lord (v 18), because he is our God, the one who brought us out of slavery in Egypt and led us into the Promised Land.

We will serve the Lord (v 21), because he is the one true God.

We will serve the Lord (v 24), because he is worthy of our heart allegiance and deserves our obedience.

Words are easy, but moments of thoughtful re-commitment like this are part of maintaining our spiritual vitality.

'So I gave you a land on which you did not toil and cities you did not build; and you live in them and eat from vineyards and olive groves that you did not plant.'
**Joshua 24:13**

## RESPOND
How would you respond if you were put on the spot like this? What are your reasons for continuing to serve God?

**Bible in a year:** Exodus 33,34; Matthew 2

# Learning to trust

## PREPARE

**As you worship God today, whether at home or with others, pray for the presence of God to be real, and the Word of God to be faithfully preached.**

## READ

Psalm 125

## EXPLORE

Some time ago, when I was deep in grief during the darkness of winter and the isolation caused by the COVID pandemic, my future seemed very bleak. I wanted to trust God but could not. My loss felt too great.

Then one day it dawned on me that it was not my ability to trust God that mattered, but the fact that he is trustworthy. Whether I could trust him or not was irrelevant, because he will always be faithful. He cannot deny himself. If we are faithless, he remains faithful (2 Timothy 2:13).

This psalm is about trust inspired by the character of God. God surrounds his people with love as surely as the mountains surround Jerusalem (v 2). We are safe because he will never leave us or forsake us. As we focus on him, and his reliability, we are able to trust him to bring us through our difficult times.

We need not fret about the wicked or those who do evil (v 3). We can leave them in God's hands. What we know is that if we are following his ways then he will continue to do good to us (v 4).

As the mountains surround Jerusalem, so the LORD surrounds his people both now and for evermore.

**Psalm 125:2**

## RESPOND

Do you find it difficult to trust, or believe you have a future? Fix your eyes on God, who is faithful. He will never abandon you or let you down. You are safe in his love.

**Bible in a year:** Exodus 35,36; Psalm 18

# In Christ alone...

There were problems in the early church. Paul had planted the group of churches in Galatia, perhaps on his first missionary journey in central or southern Turkey. All had begun well, but then he discovered they had been enticed away from the true gospel of Christ and persuaded that the old practices of Judaism were necessary as well. Paul was angry with those who had disturbed them and concerned for these young disciples.

The troublemakers had cast doubt on Paul's authority – hence his defence of his apostleship and call from God (1:11,12). This was important not just for these early believers, but for future generations' understanding of their faith in Christ. For some Jewish Christians, the practice of circumcision identified new believers as God's people. But Paul insisted that it is in Christ alone, through his cross, that we can be made children of God, members of his family.

Centuries later we may feel today that we, or at least the church leaders, have it all sorted. The issues may be different, but Paul's letter to these Christians brings us warning too. Before we feel too smug about our own understanding of the gospel, let's take a moment to think about the practices, rules and values we subtly bring to what we consider to be the correct understanding of faith. What burdens might we be laying on others? 'Watch yourself!' says Paul (6:1): 'May I never boast except in the cross of our Lord Jesus Christ' (6:14).

## About the writer
**'Tricia Williams**

'Tricia worked with Scripture Union for many years, developing and editing Bible resources. In recent years, she has been researching and writing about faith and dementia. She and her husband Emlyn live in Norfolk, where they are part of a local Anglican church.

**Monday 12 February**
Galatians 1:1–10

# Don't be a turncoat

## PREPARE
Ask God to give you courage to serve Christ alone.

. . . . . . . . . . . . . . . . . . . . . . . . . . . . . . . . . . . . . . . . . . . . . . . . . . . . .

## READ
Galatians 1:1–10

## EXPLORE
'Grace and peace to you' (v 3), Paul begins. Here is the starting point for our disagreements with other believers: we are all in relationship with God through Christ alone and are at peace with God through him. Yet, as Paul protests to these Galatian Christians, there can be no tolerance of those who would add to God's free gift of salvation (v 6).

From our perspective, we might imagine that Paul was angered by Jewish believers who wanted to impose Old Testament laws on new Gentile Christians. Paul stamps firmly on this dangerous inclination. Such teaching was saying that God's work through Jesus wasn't enough (v 7). It is imperative that the church understands salvation is through Christ alone. Today, in different ways, we may still find ourselves in danger of wanting to add to the sufficiency of Christ's gospel.

The issues we face may appear different. Yet perhaps we are also tempted to turn away from the true gospel, the completeness of God's gift in Jesus. We hear voices that persuade us to be like this or do that. It's easy to find ourselves overwhelmed by wanting to please others (v 10), rather than seeking to serve Christ alone (v 10). So, Paul pleads, don't turn away from him (v 6).

... If I were still trying to please people, I would not be a servant of Christ.
**Galatians 1:10**

## RESPOND
Sing or say to God the words of this song: 'In Christ alone my hope is found / ... / This cornerstone, this solid ground / ... / Here in the love of Christ I stand.'*

*Stuart Townend and Keith Getty, copyright © 2001, Thankyou Music

. . . . . . . . . . . . . . . . . . . . . . . . . . . . . . . . . . . . . . . . . . . . . . . . . . . . .

**Bible in a year:** Exodus 37,38; Matthew 3

# Called by God

## PREPARE
Pray: 'Lord God, help me to know that I am called by you.'

........................................................................

## READ
**Galatians 1:11–24**

## EXPLORE
I know a young woman who became a Christian a few years ago. Before her conversion, she hadn't thought much about God, and then... Everything changed, and now she is on a journey of following Christ: 'I received it by revelation from Jesus...' (v 12). Sometimes, those who observe our lives think we are merely constrained by our own opinions and don't understand that as believers we have a relationship with and are called by Christ. That's what has changed us.

Paul, met by Jesus, deliberately took time out to listen and learn from him (vs 15–21). In retrospect, he understood that he had been 'called' by God from birth (vs 15,16). His transformation from persecutor to preacher brought praise from those who witnessed this (vs 23,24) and prepared him for the ministry God had for him.

Our ministry will be different from others' (certainly Paul's!). Nevertheless, his testimony challenges us to think about our own experience of Christ. How much time are we spending deliberately with him, seeking his will and calling for our lives? Although Paul's route to faith was exceptional, notice that he didn't exclude himself from other believers (v 18). His reason for stressing his call here is to point to his dependence on Christ alone (v 11).

... when God, who set me apart from my mother's womb and called me by his grace, was pleased to reveal his Son in me so that I might preach him among the Gentiles ...

**Galatians 1:15,16**

## RESPOND
Ask God to refresh the sense of call to you and strengthen your resolve to follow him now.

........................................................................

**Bible in a year:** Exodus 39,40; Matthew 4

# Check it out

## PREPARE
Slow down. Get ready to listen to God.

..............................................................................................

## READ
**Galatians 2:1–10**

## EXPLORE
Don't rush in… You know that urgent impulse you have to tell others what you believe God is showing you? Wait. Learn from Paul.

The Galatians needed to know that Paul wasn't a crazy, rogue preacher (1:6–9). So, he tells them how (vs 1,2), after much time to reflect, he had explained his call to church leaders in Jerusalem, humbly making his case and seeking their validation (v 9). He had gone to that meeting at God's prompting (v 2) and had taken trusted others to stand with him: Titus, an uncircumcised Gentile convert, and Barnabas, whose nickname meant 'encourager' (Acts 4:36).

Titus' presence with Paul provided an important cue to explain the freedom that believers now had in Christ (vs 3–5). Significantly for the future of the young church, its leaders – James, Peter and John, once puzzled by Christ's welcome of Gentiles (eg Matthew 15:21–28; Acts 10) – now recognised and accepted Paul's message of grace to the Gentiles (vs 7–9), as Peter's call to the Jews had been (v 7). So, Paul can assure the Galatian Christians that his teaching is validated by the church leaders in Jerusalem (v 9).

'To remember the poor' may seem just an afterthought (v 10). But it was, and is, a strengthening force for uniting believers (Jew and Gentile) as the church spreads out from Jerusalem (eg Romans 15:26,27).

> … I wanted to be sure I was not running and had not been running my race in vain.
>
> **Galatians 2:2**

## RESPOND
Is there something you're impatient to do 'for God'? Pause to check out your ideas with other experienced Christians in your church.

..............................................................................................

**Bible in a year:** Leviticus 1–3;  Matthew 5

# A time to speak

## PREPARE

Pray: 'Lord, help me to know when to speak out for your truth and when to keep silent.'

· · · · · · · · · · · · · · · · · · · · · · · · · · · · · · · · · · · · · · · · · · · · · · · · · · ·

## READ

Galatians 2:11–21

## EXPLORE

Perhaps, like me, you dislike confrontation. Yet, as Paul focuses on the true gospel and its future, we see that sometimes the courage to disagree is important for unity. The issue at stake here is fundamental: the completeness of God's free gift of salvation in Jesus.

We can understand the feelings of some of those Christian Jews, arising from their tradition: they didn't eat with Gentiles because they didn't keep Old Testament laws (vs 12,13). The two-edged problem was that, in behaving like that, they were saying Christ's work was not enough – and, painfully, their actions excluded Gentile believers from the fellowship of Christ's body. Paul accused Peter (Cephas) of hypocrisy! He should have known better after his experience at the house of Cornelius (Acts 10).

We have a choice. Either we hang on to rules and discover quickly that we

can't do it! Or we accept God's gift of salvation in Christ and live in him, as he lives in us (v 20). To say that keeping the rules is important too for achieving right relationship with God is to deny the efficacy of Christ's death on the cross (v 21). Does our insistence on rule-keeping sometimes exclude other Christians from our fellowship?

I do not set aside the grace of God, for if righteousness could be gained through the law, Christ died for nothing!

Galatians 2:21

## RESPOND

Talk with God about any areas in your life where – to be honest – you are not living in line with the truth of the gospel.

· · · · · · · · · · · · · · · · · · · · · · · · · · · · · · · · · · · · · · · · · · · · · · · · · · ·

**Bible in a year:** Leviticus 4,5; Psalm 19

Galatians 3:1–14

# Faith not works

## PREPARE
Pray: 'Lord, help me not to think and live as if being a good Christian depended on my efforts.'

• • • • • • • • • • • • • • • • • • • • • • • • • • • • • • • • • • • • • • • • • • • • • • • • • • • • • • • •

## READ
Galatians 3:1–14

## EXPLORE
When you first came to Christ, you knew that your salvation depended on him alone. Filled with his Spirit, you experienced and witnessed Christ at work in you and in others around you (vs 1–5). Now, as you move on, you are perhaps beginning to think again about the old ways – and that simple security of keeping the rules (v 3). But here is the flaw in the Galatian church's thinking.

Paul points to their lack of wisdom and failure to understand the Old Testament Scriptures more deeply. Keeping the Law was never the way to salvation (vs 10,11)! It's a guide that teaches us about living God's way – and about worship and the festivals that were important in maintaining relationship with God. But we can't do it! There's a deeper truth running through God's Word which Abraham, the Jews' ancient ancestor, shows us (v 6). Right relationship with God depends on faith in him and his mercy (it's not our 'doing').

Throughout time God had a plan. The good news of the gospel for all people has always been foreseen by him (vs 8,9). The coming of Jesus and his death are the lynchpin. Now we know that Christ redeemed us through his death. Now, as Abraham's life foreshadowed, by faith we too can come into relationship with God and receive the promised blessing of his Spirit.

> So those who rely on faith are blessed along with Abraham, the man of faith.
>
> **Galatians 3:9**

## RESPOND
Ask God to refresh your faith in Christ, and to help you receive the Spirit's wisdom as you live by faith in him today.

• • • • • • • • • • • • • • • • • • • • • • • • • • • • • • • • • • • • • • • • • • • • • • • • • • • • • • • •

**Bible in a year:** Leviticus 6,7; Matthew 6

# Promise or law?

## PREPARE
Ask God to help you understand Paul's words; to grasp the difference between following God's law and receiving his promise of life in Jesus.

## READ
**Galatians 3:15–22**

## EXPLORE
Living with their Jewish heritage, it must have been hard for these Galatian believers to understand what Paul meant. Paul explains, recalling three figures that mark our faith story across millennia: Abraham, Moses ('a mediator') and Jesus Christ. These three bring different perspectives to our understanding of our relationship with God and of our faith.

Our salvation story is marked by a promise to Abraham (the covenant) (v 16). God is honouring that promise through his Seed, Jesus: 'all peoples on earth will be blessed through you' (Genesis 12:3). As we live by faith, we discover his presence with us.

However, centuries after Abraham received that prophetic promise, God's people were enslaved in Egypt. God rescues them through another giant of faith. Moses becomes the 'mediator' between God and man, receiving the Law, instigating the regime of 'you shall...' and

'you shall not...' The Law, however, does not obliterate the promise made to Abraham; rather it is given to help a wayward people live in God's ways. The giving of the covenant to Abraham and the Law to Moses both point us to the promise fulfilled in Jesus, our righteousness (v 21). We have life through faith in him (v 22).

> Is the law, therefore, opposed to the promises of God? Absolutely not! ... what was promised, being given through faith in Jesus Christ, might be given to those who believe.'
> **Galatians 3:21,22**

## RESPOND
Pray: 'Thank you, Lord, for your promises, your holy law, and your gift of life through Jesus. Help me to honour you as I live by faith in you.'

**Bible in a year:** Leviticus 8,9; Matthew 7

# 'Great things for us...'

## PREPARE
Have you had a difficult or a joyful week? Whichever, take time to meditate now on the words of this psalm.

## READ
Psalm 126

## EXPLORE
The Lord has done wonderful things for his people (v 3)! After exile and captivity in a foreign land, God brings them back to their homeland (probably around 358 BC). Now, they sing psalms of praise as they go up to worship in Jerusalem (v 2), recalling all God has done for them. So great is their praise, surrounding peoples can't help but notice and recognise the greatness of the Israelites' God. Our worship can be a witness in itself to non-believers.

Their joy bursts out; their homecoming is like a dream (vs 2,3). But then they see the reality (vs 4–6). In their absence, the land has become desolate. Yet, trusting in their faithful God, they pray for bountiful times to return – and get to work (v 4).

Despite optimism and faith, there will be no quick fixes. In reality, there will be years of hard work and tears before they see the fruit of their labours (v 6). For us too, despite the hardship and grief our troubled world brings, we can be sure: God is faithful and will bring his strength to us as we work at the tasks he has given in the here and now. Despite our tears, he will 'restore our fortunes' in unexpected ways (v 4).

> The LORD has done great things for us, and we are filled with joy.
>
> **Psalm 126:3**

## RESPOND
Bring your joys and troubles to God as you say this psalm aloud. Let his voice encourage you to praise and to work.

**Bible in a year:** Leviticus 10–12;  Psalm 20

# Children of God

## PREPARE

I am a child of God! How can this be? Ask God to help you, by his Spirit, to understand more as you read his Word today.

.........................................................................

## READ

**Galatians 3:23 - 4:7**

## EXPLORE

Good news! The guilty loads we carry are dealt with. No longer do we need to feel imprisoned by past failures (vs 23–25).

The Old Testament Law had been like a guard keeping God's people from displeasing him, teaching them to be holy but requiring sacrifice and death when they sinned (v 24). But that Law could never save people. When God sent his Son Jesus, he did something revolutionary – stepping into our shoes and taking the punishment for our sin. Faith in him brings birth into God's family (vs 25,26). Whoever you are – whatever race, status or gender (v 28) – if you belong to Christ then you are, like Abraham, a child of faith, a child of God (v 29).

The Galatian 'deserters' (1:6) were being confused by people teaching that submission to Moses' Law was necessary alongside belief in Christ.

Their false teaching left would-be Christians imprisoned by sin, denying the redeeming work of Jesus (4:4,5). No! says Paul. It's through Jesus alone, we have been made right with God, drawn into relationship with him by his Spirit (4:6). Miraculously, God has made us his children – and now, we are heirs of all the riches of our heavenly Father (4:6,7).

... God sent the Spirit of his Son into our hearts, the Spirit who calls out, '*Abba*, Father.' So you are no longer a slave, but God's child...

**Galatians 4:6,7**

## RESPOND

Thank God that in Christ you have been freed from the law of sin and death, and now you have been adopted into God's family.

.........................................................................

**Bible in a year:** Leviticus 13,14;  Matthew 8

**Tuesday 20 February**
Galatians 4:8–20

# Slavery or freedom?

## PREPARE
Pray: 'Thank you, Lord God, for the unimaginable privilege of knowing you.'

## READ
Galatians 4:8–20

## EXPLORE
Slavery or freedom? Which would you prefer? Strangely, like these young Galatian believers, we sometimes seem to prefer the false security of keeping rules (even the rules of others) and dependence on our own efforts to get things right. In doing so, we turn away from our freedom in Christ – and may influence others to do the same.

Pastor Paul is tearing his hair out with frustration and grief (vs 12,19)! The young believers had welcomed him as though he were Christ himself (v 14), caring for him through illness as he preached the gospel to them (vs 13,15). But now, they treat him as the enemy (v 16). Watch out, Paul warns. Zeal is all very well, but these intruders are self-seeking (v 17), wanting to turn the believers back to the 'weak and miserable forces' of religious laws, away from dependence on Christ (v 9). Have Paul's preaching and teaching been a waste of time (v 11)?

Paul likens his longing to see Christ (not himself) formed in them to the anguish of childbirth (v 19). It would be easier to bring warm words of commendation to the young Galatian Christians, but his love for them ('my dear children') requires a different tone (vs 19,20). The labour of the gospel can be painful.

> But now that you know God – or rather are known by God – how is it that you are turning back to those weak and miserable forces? Do you wish to be enslaved … all over again?
>
> **Galatians 4:9**

## RESPOND
Pray that you will not turn away from Christ. Pray for pastors in your church and those whom you pastor that Christ may be formed in them.

**Bible in a year:** Leviticus 15,16; Matthew 9

# Child of promise

## PREPARE

Praise God that you are a child of promise, fulfilling God's commitment made to Abraham and Sarah centuries ago.

- - - - - - - - - - - - - - - - - - - - - - - - - - - - - - - - - - - - - - - - - - - - - -

## READ

**Galatians 4:21–31**

## EXPLORE

The details of today's reading may seem complicated,* but Paul's Jewish readers would have known the history. God had promised Abraham a son with his wife, Sarah, but his relationship with his wife's slave woman (Hagar) resulted in the birth of a son, Ishmael (Genesis 16,21). Later God's promise was fulfilled in Isaac. So began the ideas of being a child of promise (Sarah) or a child of slavery (Hagar) (vs 22,23).

Paul picks out some other details from the Old Testament story. Mount Sinai (v 24) brings to mind the Law of Moses. In the light of Christ, we understand that we have been hopelessly enslaved by its rules. The city of Jerusalem (v 25) figuratively embodies people's subservience to the old covenant. Now, in Christ, we look to the Jerusalem above (v 26).

The words of verse 27 refer to the exile of God's people (Isaiah 54:1). It felt as if they had been abandoned, but God brought them back to the Promised Land – and now, in Christ, his children, born of the Spirit, are beyond number. Like Isaac, *we* are children of the promise. Don't hang on to the shackles of slavery, says Paul. That will bring contention (vs 29,30). The old ways have been superseded. Now we are to live as children of the free woman (v 31).

> Now you, brothers and sisters, like Isaac, are children of promise.
>
> **Galatians 4:28**

## RESPOND

Thank God for all he has done in your life through the power of his Spirit (v 29).

*See John RW Stott, *The Message of Galatians*, IVP, 2021, p124–126, for further help with today's Bible passage

- - - - - - - - - - - - - - - - - - - - - - - - - - - - - - - - - - - - - - - - - - - - - -

**Bible in a year:** Leviticus 17,18;  Matthew 10

# Freedom in Christ

## PREPARE
Think about what 'freedom in Christ' means for you.

∙∙∙∙∙∙∙∙∙∙∙∙∙∙∙∙∙∙∙∙∙∙∙∙∙∙∙∙∙∙∙∙∙∙∙∙∙∙∙∙∙∙∙∙∙∙∙∙∙∙∙∙∙∙∙∙∙∙∙∙∙∙∙∙∙∙∙∙∙∙∙∙∙

## READ
Galatians 5:1–15

## EXPLORE
Jewish believers were unsettling the new Gentile believers by telling them they had to be circumcised – the special, intimate sign that Jewish men were God's chosen people. But to trust in this sign of the old covenant with God was to reject the new freedom brought by Christ – in fact, Paul says, it brought a falling away from grace (v 4). To follow this disturbing teaching would mean disaster for the young churches of Galatia. No wonder Paul was so forceful in his argument!

Although so serious, Paul is careful to bring the young disciples encouragement. They had been doing so well (v 7). But he is angry with whoever has caused them to believe lies rather than the truth of Jesus who has called them (v 8). Dangerous teachings spread (v 9) and the perpetrators are to blame (v 10). Angrily (perhaps with painful wit), Paul says he wishes those who advocate this teaching might let the knives for circumcision slip (v 12)!

In our churches today, we are confronted by different issues which challenge our health and growth as believers. A righteous anger may be our reaction, but notice Paul's concern in handling this issue: 'the only thing that counts is faith expressing itself through love' (v 6).

> For in Christ Jesus neither circumcision nor uncircumcision has any value. The only thing that counts is faith expressing itself through love.
> **Galatians 5:5**

## RESPOND
Pray: 'Lord, save us from damaging the faith of others through our words and influence. Give us wisdom as we confront complex issues.'

∙∙∙∙∙∙∙∙∙∙∙∙∙∙∙∙∙∙∙∙∙∙∙∙∙∙∙∙∙∙∙∙∙∙∙∙∙∙∙∙∙∙∙∙∙∙∙∙∙∙∙∙∙∙∙∙∙∙∙∙∙∙∙∙∙∙∙∙∙∙∙∙∙

**Bible in a year:** Leviticus 19,20; Psalm 21

# In step with the Spirit

## PREPARE

As you read God's Word today, ask him to show you ways in which you are not keeping in step with the Spirit.

••••••••••••••••••••••••••••••••••••••••••••••••••••••••••••••••••••••••••••••••

## READ

Galatians 5:13-26

## EXPLORE

'Freedom' is a popular word. But people use it to mean different things. Paradoxically, the idea will always mean being in service to something or someone. In these verses, Paul draws out two opposing ideas to help the Galatian Christians understand: 'freedom' can be used selfishly to indulge our own desires of the flesh, or it can be used to love others (v 13), arising from our love for God (Matthew 22:37–40).

In the world (and in our own lives), we see conflict between selfish desire (vs 19–21) and the life of God's Spirit (v 17). However, as believers, filled by the Spirit, we are discovering freedom as our own desires begin to reflect God's desires. I am no longer under law (v 18). The fruit of the Spirit is at work in me (vs 22,23), displaying God's own love for others. But we're not there yet!

As in the early church, arguments, envy and provocation of others still threaten the community of believers (vs 15,26). Let's remember again that Christ has died for our sin (v 24). Now, given life by the Spirit, we are enabled to keep in step with the Spirit (v 25). As we love others (the Galatians needed to hear this), 'the entire law is fulfilled' (v 14).

Since we live by the Spirit, let us keep in step with the Spirit.

**Galatians 5:25**

## RESPOND

Meditate on the words of verses 22 and 23. Ask the Holy Spirit to enable you to live like this today.

••••••••••••••••••••••••••••••••••••••••••••••••••••••••••••••••••••••••••••••••

**Bible in a year:** Leviticus 21,22;  Matthew 11

# A new creation

## PREPARE
Pray: 'May I never boast except in the cross of our Lord Jesus Christ' (Galatians 6:14).

. . . . . . . . . . . . . . . . . . . . . . . . . . . . . . . . . . . . . . . . . . . . . . . . . . . . . . . . . .

## READ
Galatians 6:1–18

## EXPLORE
At the end of this letter, Paul emphasises some of his main points. We are people of the new creation, children of God, and as we learn to live by the Spirit (not the Law), there will be challenges.

First, Paul speaks to the stresses and strains of living as part of the Christian family. Things go wrong and as human beings we sin. The gentleness of the Spirit is needed as we seek in love and kindness to 'restore' one another and 'carry each other's burdens' (v 2) – that's the way to fulfil Christ's law (v 2). Watch out though! It can be easy to think we're right and we're better than others (vs 3,4)! Keep on living to please the Spirit, not the self (v 8).

Paul finishes with emphasis on the main point of his letter (v 11). The true Israel of God is made up of those who know salvation is only through the cross of Jesus. Outward signs of religiosity mean nothing (v 15). Paul has turned from the world, nailing his colours to the cross (v 14). Here he speaks God's assurance to all those who follow this way too. In living as part of God's new creation, we find peace and freedom as we trust in the grace – the undeserved mercy – of our Lord Jesus Christ (v 18).

Carry each other's burdens, and in this way you will fulfil the law of Christ.

**Galatians 6:2**

## RESPOND
Pray: 'Lord Jesus, Son of God, help me by your Spirit to live for you, trusting in you alone. Amen.'

. . . . . . . . . . . . . . . . . . . . . . . . . . . . . . . . . . . . . . . . . . . . . . . . . . . . . . . . . .

**Bible in a year:** Leviticus 23; Matthew 12; Psalm 22

# Unless the LORD...

## PREPARE

Pause... and consciously put down any worries you have about home and family before God.

. . . . . . . . . . . . . . . . . . . . . . . . . . . . . . . . . . . . . . . . . . . . . . . . . . . . . . . . . . . . . . . . . . . . .

## READ

**Psalm 127**

## EXPLORE

Our culture puts much emphasis on having a nice home, successful family and career – but what happens to our value if it's all taken away? There's a war (eg Ukraine) or an earthquake (eg Turkey and Syria) – and everything we thought gave us value, status and meaning can disappear in a moment. This psalm re-grounds our thinking in the stability brought by trust in God alone. He is the One who builds homes and gives families and security.

The first part of the psalm (vs 1,2) prompts thoughts about our twenty-first-century frantic living. We may get up early and work late into the night. Wise Solomon's words remind us that it's a waste of time unless God is in these things (v 1). In the end, he is the One who gives us peace and rest (v 2).

The second part of the psalm focuses on family (vs 3–5). If we don't have our own birth children, it may be helpful to remember that in ancient Israel families were not nuclear, but inclusive of all who lived and worshipped together (even Gentiles like us, adopted into God's family!) (Leviticus 19:34; Galatians 3:26 – 4:7). Our families are a gift from God who protect and help us as we live through the challenges of life. Today, as we worship with our church family, let's re-focus on his gifts to us and our dependence on him.

Unless the LORD builds the house, the builders labour in vain.
**Psalm 127:1**

## RESPOND

Thank God for his blessings to you and all those you love.

. . . . . . . . . . . . . . . . . . . . . . . . . . . . . . . . . . . . . . . . . . . . . . . . . . . . . . . . . . . . . . . . . . . . .

**Bible in a year:** Leviticus 24,25; Psalm 23

# Silence and song

Zephaniah's prophecies begin with a command to be silent before the Lord's destruction: people, animals, birds, fish, idols – they will all be swept away by his judgement. Is it any wonder? He lived through times of pagan and occult practices, idolatry and child sacrifices, led by kings Manasseh and Amon (2 Kings 21). As we will find out from Zephaniah's graphic descriptions of judgement, God's people had wandered far indeed.

But all was not lost. Somehow, through the few faithful servants of God left in the palace (maybe even Zephaniah himself), Amon's son Josiah followed the Lord's ways, not his father's. As he restored and repaired the Temple, a Book of the Law was discovered (probably Deuteronomy) and he embarked on ambitious reforms, removing places of idol-worship and renewing the covenant (2 Kings 22,23).

This was the world of Zephaniah. His prophecies (probably written in the mid to late seventh century BC) exposed the sin of God's people and showed them the dangerous path they were on. Perhaps they preceded Josiah's reforms; perhaps they supported them. We don't know. His glimpses of hope were fulfilled partially by those reforms, more clearly in Jesus and the cross, but fully and finally in the return of Jesus.

Zephaniah's prophecies end as they begin: with silence. Only this time God's people are listening to the love song of the Lord their God, full of joy and contentment and perfect shalom peace. Zephaniah reminds us that the Lord our God speaks words of judgement and forgiveness, holiness and love, justice and peace. Let's listen.

## About the writer
**Ben Green**

Ben is married to Jess and they live in Selly Park, Birmingham, where he is a vicar. When he isn't vicaring, Ben is most likely to be found writing computer software, but he also enjoys walking up (real) mountains, playing the piano and letting Jess plan their holidays.

# Seeking the Lord

## PREPARE

Zephaniah tells us to 'be silent' (v 7) – so let's give it a go! Focus your thoughts on God. (Perhaps picture the cross or empty tomb.) It may help to set a timer so you don't clock-watch the silence away.

. . . . . . . . . . . . . . . . . . . . . . . . . . . . . . . . . . . . . . . . . . . . . . . . . . . . . . . . . . .

## READ

**Zephaniah 1:1–13**

## EXPLORE

The beginning of Zephaniah's prophecy is breath-taking as God speaks (vs 2,3), threatening to undo his promise to Noah (see Genesis 9:15). This doesn't mean God can't be trusted to keep his promises; it is an example of prophetic hyperbole, where a prophet exaggerates to show how serious something is.

Verses 4–12 catalogue the sins of God's people – and it's quite the list. Zephaniah begins with idol worship (vs 4,5), specifically Baal (fertility cult), Molek (child sacrifice) and the stars. The people lived without reference to God (v 6), following foreign customs (v 8) and superstitions (v 9; see also 1 Samuel 5:5). God's people are supposed to be different, yet they were behaving just like everyone else.

But it's verse 12 where this prophecy hits home today. Read it again. This warning is to God's own people. How often do we live as though God 'will do nothing, either good or bad'? How often do we live as though there will be no consequences?

> 'Be silent before the Sovereign LORD.'
> **Zephaniah 1:7**

## RESPOND

Zephaniah tells us what God wants (v 6). How might you 'seek the Lord' or 'enquire of him' with all your heart, in every decision and area of your life, not only when sitting quietly with your Bible notes?

. . . . . . . . . . . . . . . . . . . . . . . . . . . . . . . . . . . . . . . . . . . . . . . . . . . . . . . . . . .

**Bible in a year:** Leviticus 26,27;  Matthew 13

# Facing the consequences

## PREPARE
What makes you really angry? Have you ever let your anger take over so you did something you now regret?

## READ
**Zephaniah 1:14 – 2:3**

## EXPLORE
The phrase the 'day of the Lord' appears first in Amos (5:18–20). God's people had looked forward to it as a day of victory and vindication, but the prophets turned that on its head: look at the way Zephaniah describes what it will actually be like in verses 15–17. His words echo what God did to Egypt centuries before, and now will do across the whole earth, including his own people. Even the tactic of buying off an invading army won't work on that day (1:18).

How do you feel when you read words like these about God's 'fierce anger' (2:2)? Do they make you shudder? Are you unsettled? Do you wonder how the same God who gave us Jesus could speak like this?

There are three things we might say. First, God's 'wrath' and 'jealousy' are not like ours: there is no malice or spite but only holiness and righteousness.

Secondly, sin is far more serious than sneaking an extra chocolate, or even cheating on your taxes: sin is us rejecting our Creator. Thirdly, even as God pronounces judgement, he offers hope to those who repent (2:1–3). There is still time.

> 'The great day of the LORD is near ... the day of the LORD's wrath.'
>
> **Zephaniah 1:14,18**

## RESPOND
Recall times when you have got really angry. If you can, confess them to God now. And don't simply say sorry. Ask God to help you change, to seek him and do what he commands (2:3). This is true repentance.

**Bible in a year:** Numbers 1; Psalms 24,25

# Righting the wrongs

## PREPARE
How do you feel when you are taunted for your faith? Or when you read a newspaper article or an online comment that mocks Jesus or your faith?

........................................................

## READ
**Zephaniah 2:4–11**

## EXPLORE
This next section does not mean judgement is only for half a dozen nations. Instead these people symbolise the whole world that rejects God and his people, in the west (vs 4–7), east (vs 8–11), south (v 12) and north (vs 13–15).

The first prophecy is to Philistia, rich in commerce and sea trade. People had built it up; now God will return it to pasture (vs 6,7). The Lord is sovereign over all: his Word pronounces judgement against all nations (v 5), no matter how far away (v 11).

The second prophecy is to Moab and Ammon (distant cousins of the Israelites via the incest of Lot's daughters: Genesis 19:30–38), for look at how they treated God's people (vs 8,10). This time the land won't be turned over to shepherds but destroyed as Sodom and Gomorrah were while Lot and his daughters fled (v 9).

Yet there is more to God's judgement than punishment. He will right all wrongs, ensure everyone faces the consequences of their actions and care for those who have been abused (vs 7,9).

> The LORD their God will care for them; he will restore their fortunes.
>
> **Zephaniah 2:7**

## RESPOND
God can take care of himself; we don't need to scream and shout, or become a crusader. Think about how you might respond graciously to someone mocking (your faith in) Jesus, perhaps by inviting them to read what Zephaniah says in verse 3.

........................................................

**Bible in a year:** Numbers 2,3;  Matthew 14

# Taking the throne

## PREPARE
Where do you see pride like Nineveh's today (v 15)? In your home, church or workplace? In yourself?

## READ
**Zephaniah 2:12–15**

## EXPLORE
Nineveh was huge. It was the capital city of the Assyrian empire, used to flaunt its leaders' wealth and power. It is said that three chariots could race around the top of its walls, they were so thick – no wonder they thought they 'lived in safety' (v 15).

However, Nineveh is perhaps most famous for being the place Jonah refused to go to – before sulking when God didn't destroy it (Jonah 1:1–3; 4:1–4). Jonah eventually got what he wanted! The repentance he saw was only temporary because Nineveh was destroyed (by the Babylonians). Around two hundred years later it was no more: desolate and dry (v 13), and returned to the animals (v 14). God's creation may suffer as a result of human sin (eg 1:3), but will also be vindicated like the 'remnant'.

What was Nineveh's crime? Aside from the horrific things it did to the nations it conquered, its sin was as old as the human race: pride (v 15). Only God can make that claim, yet nations and people keep making it for themselves. Those who don't say it out loud are often betrayed by their actions. What about you?

> She said to herself, 'I am the one! And there is none besides me.'
>
> **Zephaniah 2:15**

## RESPOND
Pride is everywhere, though it is not always as obvious as Nineveh's. How can you root out pride in your own life, and (gently) encourage an attitude of humility and service in yourself, and then elsewhere?

---

**Bible in a year:** Numbers 4,5; Matthew 15

# Heed the warning

## PREPARE

What roles do you have within your church, family, workplace, community etc? To whom are you accountable?

## READ

Zephaniah 3:1–13

## EXPLORE

After zooming out to the four corners of the world, Zephaniah focuses in on Jerusalem. He does not hold back (vs 1–8). As the godless nations were 'laid waste' (v 6), so now God's own nation will be destroyed. Don't skip past this tragedy: God's own people treat him like those who do not know him (vs 6,7).

Zephaniah condemns those responsible for leading God's people because they are corrupt and unfaithful. The officials and rulers are like ravenous animals, devouring the people instead of keeping them safe like shepherds (v 3). The prophets and priests are liars and cheats, leading God's people astray, instead of faithfully upholding the Law (v 4). But the people are no better (vs 1,2).

A few days ago (27 February) we looked at three things that help us understand and put into context God's anger. Here is a fourth: God does not punish

without warning or call to correction (vs 2,7). He even dwells within his people demonstrating righteousness and justice (v 5). But because of the sin of Nineveh (2:15; 3:11,12) he is ignored – so people face the consequences. And yet… (3:9–13).

> 'The remnant of Israel will trust in the name of the LORD.'
>
> **Zephaniah 3:12**

## RESPOND

Look again at 3:12,13. Compare that with the attitude described in verses 1–4. How can you model such a way of life day by day? Ask God for his Holy Spirit – we can't do this without his help.

**Bible in a year:** Numbers 6,7; Psalms 26,27

# Seeing the Saviour

## PREPARE
Look back over your life. What was the time of greatest joy, when you were most satisfied? Give thanks to God for that moment.

## READ
**Zephaniah 3:14–20**

## EXPLORE
The joy and excitement we feel, even in the best moments of this life, are nothing compared to the joy we will know on that day when we fully understand and know what God has done for us (vs 14,15). All God has done for us in Jesus is already true: it has already happened. On that day we will know in full and rejoice with all our hearts!

Zephaniah has guided us through some challenging home truths about our sinfulness and God's judgement and justice. But his final word is joy: not only our joy, but God's joy in us. Read again and savour verse 17 – it is precious!

How does this fit with what we've read this series? It only makes sense through Calvary (v 15). On the cross Jesus willingly took on himself the fierce anger, the wrath, the punishment we deserve, and that Zephaniah describes so graphically. Through the cross, we who

deserve death can live; we who deserve God's anger are instead his delight. In Jesus we are loved beyond measure. In Jesus we are gathered and brought home (v 20).

'God … will rejoice over you with singing.'

**Zephaniah 3:17**

## RESPOND
As I sit here and weep at the wondrous gift and love of God, I encourage you to do the same. Ask God to give you a glimpse of all he has done for you, of his great love for you, and say simply: 'Thank you.'

**Bible in a year:** Numbers 8,9; Matthew 16

# As things should be

## PREPARE
If you could be 'rich' or 'prosper' in anything, what would it be? Go on, be honest. You don't have to tell anyone!

## READ
Psalm 128

## EXPLORE
The word 'blessed' is a tricky little thing when we come across it in Psalms and Proverbs. It's easy to read verses like these in isolation and think that there is an automatic link between obedience and blessing (v 1). But that is the mistake Job's friends made: experience and the rest of the Bible tell us that the world is more complicated than that.

Psalms like this one remind us how the world should be, and one day will be: when God has removed evil and sin and brought the justice we've been reading about in Zephaniah. They are prayers, not theological essays.

But they also show us what God wants from his people: 'fear' (vs 1,4) – not 'being afraid' but showing respect and humility before our Lord, worshipping only him; 'walk in obedience' (v 1) – living life his way not 'my' way, denying ourselves for the sake of Jesus and the gospel;

'labour' (v 2) – not necessarily paid employment, but serving God faithfully wherever we find ourselves.

This psalm paints a picture of someone who maintains their focus on God without forgetting the world around. Such a person is 'whole' and 'complete' (that's what shalom peace really means – v 6). This is true blessing: true prosperity.

> May the LORD bless you from Zion.
> **Psalm 128:5**

## RESPOND
Pause for a moment and think about how you might respond to this psalm: using its words to pray blessing and peace over someone you love, or lamenting that the world is not perfect and calling God to bring his justice.

**Bible in a year:** Numbers 10,11; Matthew 17

# Apocalyptic passages in the Bible

The best known apocalyptic passages in the Bible are found in Daniel 7–12 and Revelation, along with Jesus' words in Matthew 24 and Mark 13. The prophets Isaiah (24–27), Ezekiel, Zechariah (9–14) and Joel (2,3) also used this kind of writing. The word 'apocalypse' means 'unveiling' or 'revelation', hence our book of Revelation is also sometimes called 'The Apocalypse' (the Greek word used in Revelation 1:1). But unveiling of what? And how should we approach these passages?

**Unveiling truth – present and future**

Starting further back, remember that the Bible often thinks in terms of two ages: the present age (eg 1 Corinthians 2:6–8; Galatians 1:4) and the age to come (Mark 10:30; Ephesians 2:7). The present age is characterised as 'evil' with authority wielded by 'the powers of this dark world' and 'the spiritual forces of evil in the heavenly realms' (Ephesians 6:12). The age to come sees these forces conquered and God's uncontested reign established. But the age to come is not just some distant prospect. The age to come has already invaded this age in the coming, death and resurrection of Jesus and in the forming of his body, the church. Apocalyptic passages and books in the Bible unveil this truth, warning of the destructive power of evil but pointing reassuringly to the victory of God. They fill our minds with images of peace and beauty that signal God's reign both provisionally in the present and fully in the future (eg Isaiah 65:17–25; Zechariah 8; Revelation 21). The call to God's people is to prepare to persevere in the here and now. Promoting faithful discipleship is the whole point.

**Images and symbols**

How do you go about describing this battle between forces of good and evil with its cosmic implications? Apocalyptic literature employs images, symbols (including symbolic numbers – eg '70 weeks' in Daniel, '666' in Revelation) and especially metaphors. Metaphors spark the imagination where plain statements might fail in communicating the gravity as well as the glory of what is happening. News reporters today use metaphors when they speak about 'the *war* against drugs' or a 'flood of *biblical proportions*'. They use something we know already to help us register the significance of the event. They conjure up images of a battle or Noah's flood to help us gain clearer perspective. So, John in Revelation uses a dragon to help us understand the power and impact of evil (Revelation 12). John didn't really believe in dragons! It's *like* a dragon, much as Daniel uses wild beasts to represent the machinations of world empires (Daniel 7). Another good reason for using metaphors is to avoid directly naming names, thus not tying the text down to one person or nation but enabling it to be applicable to tyrants of every age. We can tie ourselves in knots trying to link the metaphorical images to one institution or nation.

## How should we approach apocalyptic writings?

First, read them with an understanding of what type of writing they are. We should expect to work out what the images and metaphors might mean. It won't necessarily all be immediately clear, and we'll have to allow the images to move us and to ponder their significance. Don't be reluctant to seek the insight of others (without swallowing it unthinkingly).

Secondly, we should remind ourselves that we are not the first audience

for any of these passages. There was an immediate audience, and the words and images must have meant something to them. That's a good place to start. What was the point of these writings for them? What did members of the seven churches in Revelation make of the throne in heaven, the horses and the beasts? It's unlikely that it will be *entirely* different for us. A good question to ask is: How did their reading promote faithful discipleship? Then, and only then, ask how it promotes faithful discipleship for us.

Finally, try to avoid coming to these passages with preconceived notions. We may well have views on how the coming of Christ will happen and the events leading up to that great event. But try not to impose your own system on these passages. Read them carefully and let them speak to you about following Jesus.

**Writer: Andy Bathgate**

**Helpful resources:**

How to Read Apocalyptic Literature, Wendy L Widder (YouTube): https://tinyurl.com/ycksbaxs

The Bible Project, 'How to read apocalyptic literature' (YouTube): https://tinyurl.com/2p83y3xd

Ian Paul, *How to Read the Book of Revelation*, Grove Books, 2016

**A BRAND NEW SCRIPTURE UNION HOLIDAY CLUB!**

**Grab your snorkel and plunge into the book of Matthew with *Deep Sea Divers*!**

# Deep Sea Divers

Includes photocopiable resources and FREE EXTRAS online

**A Scripture Union** holiday club programme
Great new ideas inspired by experience

**Discover the depths of Jesus' love as you dive into his life, death and resurrection with children and young people.**

## FIND YOUR COPY AT: WWW.SU.ORG.UK/DEEPSEA

Also available at your local Christian bookshop

# Yes or no?

There's not much of an introduction to 1 Corinthians in the text. Paul allows himself just nine verses before he gets to business, addressing one difficult issue after another. Sometimes he answers the questions that have been sent, but more often he's responding to reports from trusted local witnesses. This letter is Paul's prophetic and pastoral challenge to the Corinthians to get back on track. Some of the issues covered in these notes are incredibly serious, but all are visceral ones that would have been deeply felt.

A key theme is God's 'no' to the culture in which they were set. Their context isn't neutral, from Paul's point of view, but a major cause of their struggles around style over substance. God says 'no' to that by choosing his weakness over human strength. Paul sees God's 'yes' in the presence and power of the Holy Spirit demonstrating the power of Christ crucified through his ministry. This is not only God's 'yes', but also the fundamental antidote to the culture's wisdom. More than this, the 'mind of Christ' which the Spirit shares with us also gives us a divine wisdom from which to discern the culture around us.

The confidence with which Paul describes God's 'no' to the culture around them is both refreshing and challenging. How discerning are we about the culture around us? To what extent might we have become too affirming of the wisdom of our culture?

## About the writer
**Mike Archer**

Mike is married to Sarah, and they have two adult children, Mims and Sam. Ordained since 1994, Mike is passionate about the renewal of the local church. He wants to know the Father well, and help others to know him too.

## Monday 4 March
### 1 Corinthians 1:1–9

# Proper perspective

## PREPARE
Read Revelation 5:11–14 and thank God for your place in his story and for his promise to be faithful all your journey through.

## READ
### 1 Corinthians 1:1–9

## EXPLORE
Before zeroing in on the issues in their church and city, Paul invites the Corinthians to look up and get a proper perspective on who they are. Reminded that they've been made holy in Jesus, they're to remember their calling to live a holy life in the world – and that they don't stand alone, for their story is part of a much bigger one involving 'all those everywhere' who belong to Jesus (v 2). Paul blesses them with God's grace and peace so that they can be fruitful in that calling (v 3).

Paul reminds them of what God has done. It began with God sending Paul to them with the gospel in the first place (v 1). So great was the outpouring of grace that they've been 'enriched in every way' (v 5). God confirmed the truth of Paul's gospel by ensuring they had every spiritual gift necessary to grow in faith (v 7). Paul's delight in them is clear: every time he prays for them

he's carried into thanksgiving for all that God has done.

The introduction ends with a reminder of what God will do. Look to the horizon, Paul insists: as you hunger to see Jesus return, depend on God's faithfulness and be sustained by fellowship with Jesus throughout the journey.

Therefore you do not lack any spiritual gift as you eagerly wait for our Lord Jesus Christ to be revealed.

**1 Corinthians 1:7**

## RESPOND
Where might spiritual gifts be lacking in you at the moment? Ask God to enrich you in every way necessary.

**Bible in a year:** Numbers 12–14; Psalms 28,29

# Tearing apart

## PREPARE
Thank God for all the ways in which you've experienced the power of Christians and local churches working together. What has God done through that unity?

## READ
1 Corinthians 1:10–17

## EXPLORE
Paul has prayed for grace and peace to come to the Corinthians, and has reminded them of what God has done and will do in and for them. On that basis he urgently (v 10) asks them to address their differences of opinion. In case they're minded to deny or downplay the situation, Paul makes clear he has a local source with both sufficient credibility to count and concern to be publicly cited (v 11). They must face it: their divisions are tearing the church apart (vs 12,13).

What's causing the divisions? Rather than seeing themselves as one church community, they were grouping with particular leaders (and possibly magnifying apparent differences between them). The language in verse 12 (literally, 'I am of Paul' and 'I am of Apollos' etc) suggests that individuals were identifying with a leader rather than with the whole church.

Worse still, from Paul's perspective, they were downplaying the significance of Jesus himself, who has somehow become just one among four leaders. They need to remember who was crucified for them. Everything they've received comes from Jesus alone, of whom the others are just heralds.

For Christ did not send me to baptise, but to preach the gospel – not with wisdom and eloquence, lest the cross of Christ be emptied of its power.

**1 Corinthians 1:17**

## RESPOND
What causes of division can you see in your local church context? How can you pray and work for unity?

**Bible in a year:** Numbers 15,16; Matthew 18

# God's 'no' to the culture

## PREPARE
How easy would you find it to buy a cheaper coffee or less stylish clothes? How much does the image of something matter to you?

## READ
**1 Corinthians 1:18 – 2:5**

## EXPLORE:
Greek culture had rules by which it evaluated arguments (called rhetoric). These rules governed how an argument was put together and also what it should sound like. An elegant, well-constructed argument was considered wise and, therefore, convincing.

But Paul has no interest in making the gospel 'wise' in those terms. Neither, he thinks, does God. Why otherwise would God have chosen those without education, influence or nobility to further the gospel (vs 26–29)? God has chosen those the culture despises to be his advocates, intending that none can boast before him. God is saying 'no' to human cultures and their claim to wisdom.

Given this, Paul set out to make God's argument for Jesus on God's terms. He refused the wisdom of rhetoric, resisting the use of eloquence (2:1). While with them, Paul determined only to know

'Jesus Christ and him crucified' (2:2). Depending on the Spirit to authenticate his words (2:4,5), he set out to found their faith on God's power being demonstrated, rather than rhetoric. That is divine wisdom: Christ crucified (2:2) and the power and wisdom of God (1:24).

> My message and my preaching were not with wise and persuasive words, but with a demonstration of the Spirit's power.
>
> **1 Corinthians 2:4**

## RESPOND
Read John 16:8–11. Ask the Holy Spirit to convince you of any areas where you're not hearing God's 'no' to the culture around you. Thank God for the gift of Christ, 'the power … and the wisdom of God' (1:24).

**Bible in a year:** Numbers 17–19; Matthew 19

# Into the depths

## PREPARE
Read Romans 8:14–16. Ask the Holy Spirit to share with your spirit a conviction that you are God's child. Pray for others you know to experience this too.

## READ
**1 Corinthians 2:6–16**

## EXPLORE
God's rejection of human wisdom and culture is more than a 'no'. It's an invitation to understand that we can know God.

Partly this is about us knowing the 'mystery' of salvation, grasping through the Spirit all that God has graciously given us (vs 7,12). Human wisdom, which can't or won't understand (v 14), has to give way to divine wisdom which redefines reality for us (vs 7,14). This is revealed – not discovered – as the Holy Spirit within us interprets 'spiritual realities' in words that the Spirit must first teach us (v 13). Our faith rests on what's been revealed to us rather than what human wisdom can discover or construct.

But even more than this we're privileged to know not just what God has done, but to know God himself. Paul boldly claims that we can know a measure of the depths of God through the presence within us of the Holy Spirit, God's very self (vs 10–12). That means we can know something of the thoughts of God, which Paul calls the 'mind of Christ' (v 16). This astounding privilege no human culture or wisdom can ever give to us. That's why we must rest on Christ crucified alone.

> For who knows a person's thoughts except their own spirit within them? In the same way no one knows the thoughts of God except the Spirit of God.
>
> **1 Corinthians 2:11**

## RESPOND
Bring any matters about which you need to discern the mind of Christ to God (v 15). Ask God to speak by his Holy Spirit.

**Bible in a year:** Numbers 20,21;  Matthew 20

# No more than servants

## PREPARE
Pray for church leaders you know to have a proper humility and a sense of ease in their calling.

• • • • • • • • • • • • • • • • • • • • • • • • • • • • • • • • • • • • • • • • • • • • • • • • • • • • • • • • • •

## READ
**1 Corinthians 3:1–23**

## EXPLORE
The Corinthians thought they'd arrived (see 1 Corinthians 4:8), but Paul insists they're not even spiritually weaned (v 2). Why? Because their divisions are tearing the church apart (vs 16,17), dishonouring the Spirit's presence in their midst. Internal strife focused on leaders is showing just how much they've bought into worldly wisdom (v 3). They're mistaking the servants for the Source (v 5).

They have to see leaders from the right perspective. Called by God's grace (v 10), they're significant in God's purpose as God's 'fellow workers'. But they should be given no special dignity beyond their place in God's purpose (v 9). God grows the church, with leaders simply serving God in that endeavour (v 8), building on the foundation of Jesus Christ (v 11).

The very things the Corinthians most value – the stylishness of rhetoric – don't matter to Paul. All that matters is whether what's built matches the foundation. One that's true to the foundation will come unscathed through the Refiner's Fire (vs 12–15). Both the followers and their leaders need to be careful: if they're dishonouring the Spirit's presence in their midst by pursuing quarrels, they will face judgement (vs 16,17). They must remember the pre-eminence of Christ – not one leader among many, but the only source of grace (vs 11,23).

> Don't you know that you yourselves are God's temple and that God's Spirit lives among you?
>
> **1 Corinthians 3:16**

## RESPOND
Reflect on any tensions within your relationships or within your local church. Are you contributing to them? Or helping to resolve them?

• • • • • • • • • • • • • • • • • • • • • • • • • • • • • • • • • • • • • • • • • • • • • • • • • • • • • • • • • •

**Bible in a year:** Numbers 22,23; Psalm 30

# Kingdom thinking

## PREPARE
Reflect on your sense of calling. Where are you being fruitful? Where might you need a fresh empowerment from the Spirit?

## READ
**1 Corinthians 4:1–21**

## EXPLORE
Paul uses two humble terms to describe leaders in verse 1: 'servants' and stewards. The word used for the first suggests someone who works with his hands. The stewards (the ones 'entrusted') own nothing, yet take care of all their master's property (v 2). It seems that Paul's ministry was being openly challenged, but he is content to leave the question of his faithfulness to the owner of the household alone (vs 3–5). Paul challenges the local leaders not to get boastful about either Apollos or himself (v 6). All of them are but servants of the Lord (v 1).

Such is their confidence the Corinthians believe they're already reigning, experiencing heaven on earth (v 8), but Paul reminds them that everything they're boasting about was received from others (v 7). In fact, as the one who laid the foundation (see 1 Corinthians 3:10,11), he should be honoured both as their father in God (vs 14,15) and in his struggles to live for Jesus, responding in grace to others, despite real hardship and opposition (vs 11–13).

In the end, it's the presence of God's power, not the beauty of the words that should be decisive (vs 19,20). That's how the presence of God's kingdom is truly discerned.

> For the kingdom of God is not a matter of talk but of power.
>
> **1 Corinthians 4:20**

## RESPOND
Read verse 20 again. Where would you say that we in the modern church are more concerned with style than with God's power?

**Bible in a year:** Numbers 24,25;  Matthew 21

# Together on the road

## PREPARE
Today is Mothering Sunday in the UK. Thank God for all that you've received from your mother and your family, wherever you are! Where others have filled up what was missing, thank God for them.

## READ
Psalm 129

## EXPLORE
This psalm is one of the processional songs used by pilgrims on their way to Jerusalem. The first four verses function more like a creed or a testimony than a prayer. The phrase 'Let Israel say' (v 1) is in the mouth of a service leader, encouraging those on pilgrimage to join in: together they are Israel, and while their story has been one of opposition and struggle, no enemy has ever gained final victory. They remain a people sustained by God's presence and justice. In spite of others' determination to make them suffer (v 3), God has cut them free (v 4).

Ascending to the heights of Zion, the heart of their nation and its faith, the psalm becomes a prayer that all who wish to oppress Israel will be turned back in defeat (v 5); that they will be like a failed harvest (vs 6–8a). In contrast, the concluding lines declare blessing (v 8) on God's people, who have a special relationship with the Lord, as they remember their own place in Israel's story.* Remember today how God has blessed you, your family and your church.

> 'But the LORD is righteous; he has cut me free from the cords of the wicked.'
>
> Psalm 129:4

## RESPOND
Together we are a chosen people (1 Peter 2:9,10). Ask for a greater sense of community and togetherness as you praise God today and thank him for his blessings on you.

*See Michael Wilcock, *The Message of Psalms*, IVP, 2001

**Bible in a year:** Numbers 26,27; Matthew 22

# Stopping the rot

## PREPARE

Invite the Holy Spirit to show you whether there are any specific situations, sins or attitudes that are making it hard for you to hear God at the moment.

## READ

**1 Corinthians 5:1–13**

## EXPLORE

A serious report has reached Paul: a church member is in a continuing liaison with his father's wife. Even the unshockable Greeks would be scandalised by such a sexual relationship (vs 1,2). Paul wants to know how it is that they're not grieved by this. The unholiness must be removed from the church as old yeast from the dough (vs 6,7,13). The fact that they haven't sensed God's grief at this suggests they're already becoming spiritually dulled. They must stop the rot. They have no reason for pride or boasting (vs 2,6).

Paul's language in verses 3–5 is hard to grasp. Through their fellowship in the Spirit, Paul expects to exercise his authority in some present sense by the Spirit's power even while absent. Perhaps what's meant is that, as Paul's judgement is read out as they're gathered to worship, the power of the Lord Jesus will convince those present.

They need to redraw some boundaries (not just about sex). They're to stop breaking bread with those claiming to be following Jesus if they won't address persistent patterns of sinful behaviour. Just as with the first man (v 1), they're to break fellowship with such people, intending to draw them back to God in penitence (vs 5,10,11).

... let us keep the Festival, not with the old bread leavened with malice and wickedness, but with the unleavened bread of sincerity and truth.

**1 Corinthians 5:8**

## RESPOND

Reflect on how you are drawing boundaries at the moment. In what ways might the Lord want you to redraw them?

**Bible in a year:** Numbers 28,29;  Psalm 31

## Tuesday 12 March
### 1 Corinthians 6:1–11

# Do you not know?

## PREPARE

Pray for all those who have not found justice or safety within the church. Ask for God's forgiveness for all those times when we haven't lived up to our calling.

---

## READ

**1 Corinthians 6:1–11**

## EXPLORE

From Paul's perspective, the Corinthian Christians' divisions undermine their claim to maturity. Some conflicts are so bitter they've ended up in the state courts. Three times Paul uses the same question to show what a disaster this is: 'Do you not know?' (vs 2,3,9).

The first truth they should know is that the Lord's people will judge the world, including the angels (vs 2,3). So how can those who will judge the world ask the world for justice? Especially not in trivial matters. Better, Paul insists, that we accept being wronged than humiliate the Lord's people like this.

Worse still, their actions show no confidence that such a matter can be handled fairly within the church. If that's the case, how present is the Spirit who gives them access to the mind of Christ (2:16)? These disputes, ending up before the secular authorities, show their complete defeat (v 7).

As dire as all this is, the second truth Paul insists they should remember is what God has done in them: they have been washed, sanctified and justified in Jesus and by the Spirit (v 11). They must remember these truths and resolve again to receive and live them out.

> ... But you were washed, you were sanctified, you were justified in the name of the Lord Jesus Christ and by the Spirit of our God.
>
> **1 Corinthians 6:11**

## RESPOND

Read Romans 12:18. Where might God be calling you to be a peacemaker in your family or local church?

---

**Bible in a year:** Numbers 30,31; Matthew 23

# Body matters

## PREPARE
Read Psalm 139:13–18 and thank God for your body, fearfully and wonderfully made.

. . . . . . . . . . . . . . . . . . . . . . . . . . . . . . . . . . . . . . . . . . . . . . . . . . . . . . . . . . . . . . . . . . . . . . . .

## READ
**1 Corinthians 6:12–20**

## EXPLORE
Paul now challenges the Corinthians' teaching. He quotes two of their slogans, which asserted complete spiritual freedom (v 12) and that the body has no lasting spiritual significance because it's going to be destroyed (v 13).

Paul emphasises his opposition by repeating 'Do you not know?' a further three times (vs 15,16,19). He stresses that the resurrection of Jesus is bodily and that, therefore, ours will be too (v 14). That means it simply cannot be the case that what we do with our bodies doesn't matter to the Lord (vs 19,13). Yes, we're free in Christ, but don't, Paul insists, draw the wrong conclusion: freedom isn't licence to do as we please (see Galatians 5:13). We can damage ourselves and find ourselves trapped anew (v 12).

That's why avoiding the sexual immorality around them matters. The Corinthians are united to Christ in their bodies, which are temples of the Holy Spirit (v 19). If they sleep with a prostitute, they form a one-flesh relationship with that person. They're invited to imagine uniting Christ to that prostitute. That cannot be ('Never!', v 15). That's why they must flee from sexual immorality (v 18). They're sinning against the place where they will experience Christ's final victory. Given the costliness of that victory (v 20), they must honour God with their bodies.

> By his power God raised the Lord from the dead, and he will raise us also.
>
> **1 Corinthians 6:14**

## RESPOND
Read John 8:10,11. This is an area where we easily feel guilt, yet Jesus offers both forgiveness and a challenge. Which is most relevant for you?

. . . . . . . . . . . . . . . . . . . . . . . . . . . . . . . . . . . . . . . . . . . . . . . . . . . . . . . . . . . . . . . . . . . . . . . .

**Bible in a year:** Numbers 32,33; Matthew 24

# Freedom isn't licence

## PREPARE

In what areas do you find self-control difficult? Ask for God's strength and mercy.

..........................................................

## READ

1 Corinthians 7:1–16

## EXPLORE

Having challenged them about incest and using prostitutes, Paul now starts addressing the Corinthians' questions (v 1). If the body and sexual sin matter, as he's arguing, can sex ever be a good thing? Isn't it better to abstain altogether?

Paul recognises the desire to have an undivided focus on the Lord (see 7:32), but he regards celibacy as a specific gift and calling (v 7). Trying to live that out when it's not your calling will cause grief (v 9). Instead, Paul argues that marriage is an important gift in such a promiscuous culture (v 2). In balanced language, wives and husbands are given authority over their spouse's bodies: they're to be different from the culture around them by meeting each other's sexual desires within marriage (vs 2–4). Yes, they can abstain, but only for a time to deepen their spiritual lives and if they both agree (v 5). Then they must come together again so that their desire to be devoted to the Lord isn't undermined by temptation.

Paul's concern throughout is pastoral, balancing concessions and commands (vs 6,10,12) and making wise, practical decisions to limit harm in a messy world where faith and unbelief coexist, even in our homes (vs 10–16).

> I wish that all of you were as I am. But each of you has your own gift from God; one has this gift, another has that.
>
> **1 Corinthians 7:7**

## RESPOND

Pray for both the married couples and the single people close to you. Ask for God's blessing on them in their different callings. Pray also for those experiencing separation and divorce.

..........................................................

**Bible in a year:** Numbers 34,35;  Matthew 25

# Fruitful wherever

## PREPARE
Monks and nuns swear an oath of stability: to stay in the same place unless called otherwise. To what extent do you feel a call to where you're living at the moment?

## READ
1 Corinthians 7:17–24

## EXPLORE
Although it's translated 'live', Paul often describes discipleship as a walk (v 17). Answering God's call to obey is the priority (v 19).

Why? Because we've been bought at a price, ie 'bought in the (slave) market' (v 23; see also 1 Corinthians 6:20). Once slaves to sin, now the One who has redeemed us has the right to dictate our steps (Romans 6:17,18). That's why obeying the Lord has priority over changing our circumstances (v 19). Even those who were legally free (v 22) must see themselves as Christ's slaves, and those who are slaves as his freed people (although Paul encourages escaping slavery legally, verse 21). No human leader should be given the place that belongs to Jesus alone (v 23).

What makes the difference is that God is with us. The language of verses 20 and 24 is very similar in Greek.

They both read, 'Each one in the calling in which he was called, let him remain.' But the phrase 'with God' is added in verse 24 (see NRSVA). The reality of God's presence and power can transform us in and within our circumstances, making us fruitful for God wherever we find ourselves.

> You were bought at a price; do not become slaves of human beings.
>
> **1 Corinthians 7:23**

## RESPOND
Ask God to show you how he is with you and how you can be fruitful wherever he has planted you.

**Bible in a year:** Numbers 36; Deuteronomy 1; Psalm 32

# What serves holiness?

## PREPARE

Pray for those you know struggling with their singleness or their relationships at the moment. Ask for God's mercy and grace to be at work, bringing peace to households.

## READ

1 Corinthians 7:25–40

## EXPLORE

Paul's concern here is both pastoral and practical. Without a specific command from the Lord, Paul trusts to God's mercy and his own discernment to give wise advice (vs 25,40). Paul's challenge is that the Corinthians want clarity in choosing between two outcomes that are both good. Paul's response can best be summed up as asking the question, 'What best serves holiness?'

The context isn't clear. It might be there was an imminent expectation that the Lord would return (v 29: 'the time is short'), but the 'present crisis' (v 26) might suggest a local context (perhaps the unexpected deaths referred to in 1 Corinthians 11:27–32). That second background would change the advice to remain unmarried into advice to wait until the crisis has passed.

Against that background, Paul recommends celibacy because an unmarried person has fewer concerns that pull them away from an 'undivided devotion' to the Lord's purposes (v 35). While being a spouse and a parent are both undeniably good things, they're inevitably distracting (vs 33,34). Choosing to marry rather than remain unmarried is not choosing wrongly, but Paul dares to say that choosing celibacy is even better because it best serves holiness (v 38).

> I am saying this for your own good, not to restrict you, but that you may live in a right way in undivided devotion to the Lord.
>
> **1 Corinthians 7:35**

## RESPOND

'Undivided devotion' (v 35) sets a high bar for all of us. What steps towards this could you take?

**Bible in a year:** Deuteronomy 2,3; Matthew 26

# Waiting and longing

## PREPARE
Remember those you know who are waiting and longing at the moment. Listen to God for them, and, if appropriate, share what you believe God might be saying.

## READ
Psalm 130

## EXPLORE
Whatever the original setting of the psalm, it's become one of the processional songs used by pilgrims on their way to Jerusalem for the feasts. As such, it captures the longing of the people to meet with God and know his presence and blessing.

The writer is in turmoil (v 1), giving the whole psalm a passionate intensity. His urgent request to be heard (v 2) is followed by the recognition that he doesn't deserve to be standing before God (v 3). Yet the demand is pressed anyway because forgiveness is inherent in God's character (v 4). The psalmist looks once again to serve God reverently after receiving forgiveness and mercy. But no resolution comes. The intensity of his longing simply builds – his whole being waiting, staking his trust on God's word and character (v 5). Greater even than the longing of the night guards for the coming of the dawn is his longing for an assurance of God's forgiveness and renewed favour (vs 5,6).

At the end of the psalm, those ascending to the feast are invited to make the writer's impassioned song their own (vs 7,8). What mercy are they seeking as they put their hope once again in the God of Israel?

> I wait for the LORD, my whole being waits, and in his word I put my hope.
>
> **Psalm 130:5**

## RESPOND
Read Psalm 46:10. Be still and bring anything you're waiting on God about into his presence. Remember to extol him and ask for a breakthrough.

**Bible in a year:** Deuteronomy 4,5; Matthew 27

# A word to the wise

**About the writer**
**Jennie Pollock**

Jennie Pollock is a writer and editor. She is the author of *If Only: Finding joyful contentment in the face of lack and longing.* Her website is jenniepollock.com

Wisdom can be a tricky thing to define, though we can probably all think of people we consider wise. Perhaps 'applied knowledge' is a good way of describing it.

In this series of readings we will be looking at some of the wisdom Solomon wrote down for his son. In these early chapters of Proverbs, however, there is less practical wisdom and more exhortation to pursue wisdom – less of the 'what' and more of the 'why'.

Solomon was, famously, the king who asked God for wisdom instead of wealth or power or anything else he might have wished for. This was in itself a wise request, showing a deep level of understanding of the task facing him, and a humility to recognise he would need God's help to carry it out. In this book we find him trying to pass on his wisdom to his son – and to any of us who will listen.

He uses every rhetorical device he can think of to try to drive his point home – warning of the dangers of folly, promising the rewards of wisdom, enticing us with images of wisdom's beauty, threatening us with the consequences of evil. Wisdom, he is telling us, is really important. Whatever else you do in life, be sure that you get wisdom.

His passion is contagious. As you read, try to hear and catch Solomon's enthusiasm for his topic. And ask God to help you care about it as much as he does: 'The fear of the Lᴏʀᴅ is the beginning of wisdom' (Proverbs 9:10; 1:7).

# Wisdom's beauty

## PREPARE
As we begin a week of thinking about wisdom, reflect on some wise people you know or have known in your life.

## READ
Proverbs 1:1–19

## EXPLORE
How do we grow in wisdom? And why would we want to? These are some of the questions Solomon begins to deal with in this appeal to his son.

Some of the 'how' is encapsulated in today's key verse: by paying attention to the teachings of your parents. This is a counter-cultural statement in the twenty-first century when expectation is often that young people must find their own path and embrace the truth they find inside themselves. People of older generations tend to be considered out of touch, unable to understand the pressures on young people today.

Verse 7 pulls no punches when it declares, 'fools despise wisdom and instruction'. No one wants to be thought a fool, surely. Then verse 9 adds some 'carrot' to verse 7's 'stick': instruction and teaching from the wise will beautify you. They will adorn your life like fine jewellery and garlands of flowers. Wise people often are attractive in character, aren't they? Their wisdom permeates everything they say and do, including the ways they interact with others. It makes them a pleasure to be around. Solomon wants us to recognise that beauty and to desire it. This will be an antidote to the enticements to folly he outlines in the rest of the passage.

Listen, my son, to your father's instruction ... do not forsake your mother's teaching. They are a garland to grace your head and a chain to adorn your neck.
Proverbs 1:8,9

## RESPOND
Ask God to help you grow in the beauty of wisdom. Thank him for the wise guides he has put into your life.

**Bible in a year:** Deuteronomy 6,7; Psalm 33

97

# Why won't they listen?

## PREPARE
Ask God to help you tune out the distractions around you and listen for his voice as you read his Word today.

........................................................

## READ
**Proverbs 1:20–33**

## EXPLORE
Wisdom is personified in today's passage as a woman roaming the streets, calling out for anyone to hear her. Perhaps you might picture her as a street preacher, desperately trying to interest people in the gospel. Or these days she might be depicted on social media, trying to speak truth into the cacophony of angry, misleading or time-wasting posts.

Wherever you picture her, you can sense her frustration as she watches people pursue foolish ends in foolish ways. She longs for them to turn from their folly, but ultimately everyone has to make their own choices.

Verses 24–31 sound shocking, as those reaping the consequences of their poor choices ask for help too late. Yet the Bible repeatedly urges us to ensure that we are right with God – the very bedrock of wisdom – while we have time (eg Isaiah 55:6; Matthew 7:21–27; 25:1–13).

In Genesis 7 there came a point when God shut the door of Noah's ark and those who refused to heed his call were left outside. In the same way, there will come a day when we run out of time to act wisely. Let us turn and listen to wisdom while we still can.

'How long will you who are simple love your simple ways? How long will mockers delight in mockery and fools hate knowledge?'
**Proverbs 1:22**

## RESPOND
Pray: 'Father, thank you that you love to give wisdom to any who will listen. Forgive me when I close my ears to you. Help me to turn from my foolish ways and walk in your wisdom. Amen.'

........................................................

**Bible in a year:** Deuteronomy 8,9;  Matthew 28

# A gift worth seeking

## PREPARE
Think of a time when you pursued a worthwhile goal. How did you feel during the process and when it was complete?

## READ
**Proverbs 2:1–22**

## EXPLORE
There is a paradox in today's passage. Verse 6 tells us wisdom is a gift from the Lord, but verses 1–5 suggest that we have to work for it. Look at all the verbs in those verses: accept, store up, turn, apply, look, search. They don't depict someone who acquires wisdom accidentally, who just wakes up one day and finds they are wise! There are things we can and must do in order to grow in wisdom.

But we can be assured that it won't be a fruitless search. James 1:5 tells us that God gives wisdom generously to anyone who asks for it, and verse 5 of today's passage promises that the seeker will find. It promises other rewards too. Wisdom and understanding will protect you from wicked people and from sexual temptation and will bring you success. We will look more at this theme tomorrow, but for now just note that the effort will be rewarded.

How do we pursue this wisdom then? Studying God's Word (including this book, which many people find tricky!); spending time with wise, godly people, listening to them and learning from their lives; reading Christian biographies and teaching materials. Seek these things out, and God will use them to give you wisdom (vs 1–6).

> For the LORD gives wisdom; from his mouth come knowledge and understanding.
>
> **Proverbs 2:6**

## RESPOND
What will you do to pursue wisdom in the next few days? Ask God to point you in the right direction.

**Bible in a year:** Deuteronomy 10,11;  Romans 1

# Healthy, wealthy and wise?

## PREPARE
What are you longing for in your life? Has it ever occurred to you to desire wisdom? Does wisdom seem precious to you?

..............................................................................

## READ
**Proverbs 3:1–18**

## EXPLORE
Solomon is working really hard to 'sell' wisdom and its benefits in today's passage. He wants his son (and us) to pursue it, so he uses these verses to speak of its rewards. Obeying God's commands and putting him first, he says, will bring long life, good health, riches, honour, peace and more (v 2)!

This can be hard to believe when we see godly people suffering and wicked people thriving, when faithful believers die young and corrupt leaders gain wealth and honour. How can we reconcile the words of the Bible with what we see playing out around us?

We have to remember that this life is only a small part of the story. There's something much bigger going on – something eternal. Other biblical passages, such as Psalm 73, remind us to lift our gaze from this earthly moment and see the big picture. It might seem

as though the wicked 'have no struggles' (Psalm 73:4) and that godly wisdom is not worth the effort, but one day God will bring justice to all (2:22).

God's word can be trusted (v 5). Pursuing wisdom will bring his people all these promised rewards at just the right time: 'Those who hold fast will be blessed' (v 18).

> Blessed are those who find wisdom, those who gain understanding.
>
> **Proverbs 3:13**

## RESPOND
Do you need God's help to hold fast to his promises just now? Do you know others who are struggling with doubt? Ask God for his strength and help for all who need it.

..............................................................................

**Bible in a year:** Deuteronomy 12–14; Romans 2

# Have you got it yet?

## PREPARE

Pray: "'I have hidden your word in my heart that I might not sin against you" (Psalm 119:11). Lord, help me to hear, remember and heed your words.'

## READ

Proverbs 4:1–9

## EXPLORE

'Mind how you cross the road!' As my brother and I grew old enough to walk to school or the shops on our own, Mum would call this after us every time we left the house. It grew to be such a habit that she did it once by accident when I was visiting from university! The things we hold to be of utmost importance we repeat over and over again.

These verses feel rather like that, don't they? As if the last three chapters of warning, cajoling and exhorting haven't been enough, Solomon once again instructs his son, 'Get wisdom.'

Look at the different relationships he mentions to drive his point home. He himself learned wisdom from his parents (David and Bathsheba), as well as the importance of wisdom. He in turn is seeking to pass these lessons on to his son. Verses 6–9 again depict wisdom as a woman – and this time using quite romantic language (love, cherish, embrace). Through these images wisdom is being associated – in the son's mind and ours – with love, nurture, passion and desire.

> The beginning of wisdom is this: get wisdom. Though it cost you all you have, get understanding.
>
> **Proverbs 4:7**

## RESPOND

What do you think the costs might be, that Solomon hints at in verse 7? How might it be costly to pursue wisdom and understanding? Ask God to help you value wisdom as highly as Solomon did, and to seek it at any price.

**Bible in a year:** Deuteronomy 15,16; Psalm 34

# Watch your step!

## PREPARE
Pray this verse as you settle your heart today: 'Show me your ways, Lord, teach me your paths. Guide me in your truth and teach me' (Psalm 25:4,5).

## READ
**Proverbs 4:10–27**

## EXPLORE
A friend and I recently saw a play set in 1930s Germany. The main character was an academic who was approached by some Nazi leaders and asked to write a paper for them. Flattered, he agreed. Yet this seemingly small act started him on a path which got harder and harder to leave. Eventually, this generally good man became a Nazi agent, simply by taking dozens of tiny steps away from his principles. Each one caused him to hesitate, but each time he moved forward.

That is the danger Solomon is warning against here. Once you set a single foot on the road that wicked people follow, you will quickly find yourself walking along it (vs 14,15). Turn away while you have the chance.

Verses 16 and 17 depict wickedness almost like an addiction: evildoers can't get any rest until they have done evil.

It's a compulsion, driving them further and further down the path. The 'first steps' become like a 'gateway drug' – something that seems mild, but that quickly leads to experimentation with more, and more deadly, things. As the old anti-drug adverts used to say, 'Just say no!'

> Give careful thought to the paths for your feet and be steadfast in all your ways.
> **Proverbs 4:26**

## RESPOND
To stay on the path of wisdom, we have to fix our eyes on the destination and choose to walk towards it. Ask God to help you set your eyes on him and walk steadfastly in his ways.

**Bible in a year:** Deuteronomy 17,18; Romans 3

# A reign of peace

## PREPARE

Today is Palm Sunday. As you read today's passage, try to picture the scene – the sights, sounds and smells. Engage your emotions as well as your brain.

## READ

**John 12:12–16**

## EXPLORE

Why did Jesus enter Jerusalem on a donkey (v 15)? Surely such a beast is too humble for a king? Nowadays we hold donkeys in low esteem, but in the ancient Middle East they were a common mode of transport for those who could afford them. In 1 Kings 1:32–45 we read of David, at the end of his life, commissioning Zadok and Nathan to proclaim Solomon as the new king. David tells them to place Solomon on David's own mule for the journey to the place of anointing.

Horses were used back then more commonly in war, whereas donkeys were associated with peace. Verse 15 of today's reading is a quotation from Zechariah 9:9,10. The first of these verses contains the prophecy about Israel's king riding on a donkey, but the second explains that one of the things this king will do is to remove the war horses from Jerusalem.

When Jesus rode into the city on this donkey, he was acting as a king who came in peace. And we can be assured that there will be a day when he will come in peace again. His enemies will be defeated, and he will rule for ever.

> 'Do not be afraid, Daughter Zion; see, your king is coming, seated on a donkey's colt.'
>
> **John 12:15**

## RESPOND

Pray: 'Lord Jesus, you are the true king, who comes to rule in peace. We praise you and worship you. We long for the day when you return in glory and majesty. Come, Lord Jesus! Amen.'

**Bible in a year:** Deuteronomy 19,20;  Romans 4

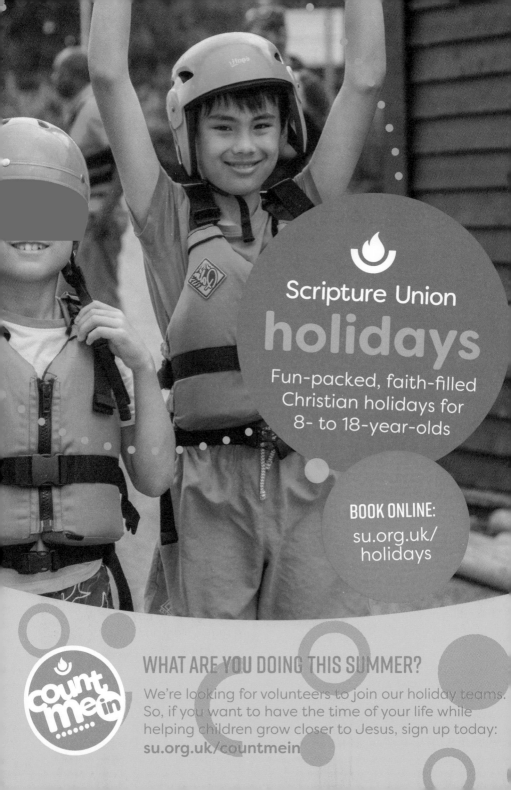

# The true and the new

John's account of the hours leading up to Jesus' death and the days immediately following his resurrection takes up nearly half his Gospel. The chapters preceding these show us, through his teaching and prayers (John 13–17), the priorities that Jesus longed to leave with his followers. Concluding that time, Jesus starts his final journey towards the cross and – looking over John's shoulder – we join him.

In narrating events, John's writing is rich with recurring themes, meaningful contrasts, stark irony and eyewitness details. His stated purpose (20:31) is to engender life-giving belief in the truth of who Jesus is. These chapters highlight Jesus as the true Shepherd, true High Priest, true Passover Lamb, true Son of the Father, true King, true Adam, and Truth Himself. Another theme to look out for, especially in the second half of our series, is the newness that opens out of the empty tomb: new life, new faith, new peace, new purpose, new perspective, new calling, new wholeness – to name but a few! What truth about who he is might Jesus want to reveal to you this Easter? What newness might he be waiting to lead you into?

As we come to contemplate the Passion, let me invite you to ask God for the grace to be present to Jesus in his suffering, to 'sorrow with Christ in sorrow' (Ignatius Loyola), allowing that to deepen your walk with and love for him.

## About the writer
### Cath Butler

Cath enjoys working as a peripatetic music tutor, and she has just qualified as a spiritual director. Her primary 'love languages' are the clarinet, pancakes, walks by the sea, reading and journaling. She writes for and edits @PilgrimsPages – a social media hub designed to help people explore journaling as a spiritual practice.

## Monday 25 March
John 18:1–14

# Who are you seeking?

## PREPARE
Do you have a place where you often meet with God? Remember significant times with him in that place.

## READ
**John 18:1–14**

## EXPLORE
In deepest darkness, the disciples' safe and familiar place of fellowship with Jesus is disturbed. Man-made lights emphasise their carriers' spiritual night as violence comes to arrest peace. Echoes of another God-frequented garden (Genesis 2,3) stir in our memories as, once again, humankind betrays God's friendship. But this time, it is man looking for God in the garden, and the One who is sought steps forward rather than hiding (v 4).

John's repetition (vs 4,7) draws our attention to a theme that is central to his Gospel, and the pivot upon which these pages of history turn: Who is this man you seek? Judas' band of soldiers and religious leaders thought they were looking for a dissenter and are stunned by Jesus' revelation of deity – 'I am he' (vs 5,6,8; see also John 8:58). But they are not deterred (v 12). Who do you want when you seek after Jesus? How often is the One we see – and how we respond – clouded by our own preconceptions and purposes?

Calmly in control at the centre of the storm, the true Shepherd shields his flock from the suffering he is about to undergo (vs 8,9), rerouting their expectations and repairing the damage caused by their attempts to get there, unwavering in both his mission and means of accomplishing it.

Jesus, knowing all that was going to happen to him, went out and asked them, 'Who is it you want?'
**John 18:4**

## RESPOND
Honestly tell Jesus who you are wanting him to be today, then ask him to reveal more of himself to you.

**Bible in a year:** Deuteronomy 21,22; Psalm 35

# 'I am not'

## PREPARE
Pray: 'Lord God, thank you for all you have made and called me to be. Forgive me when I hide that, and please lead me into its fullness.'

## READ
**John 18:15-27**

## EXPLORE
Divine deliverance bound, and heaven's high priest interrogated by his human counterpart – this is the scene John now sets before us (v 15). How did Peter and John ('another disciple', v 15, most likely one of several third-person self-identifications by the Gospel's author) feel following Jesus into the official residence of the religious patriarchy? The fierce, perhaps older fisherman kept outside until his well-connected friend could persuade a servant girl to let him in... the master who had led them, now following his arresters... and the hostile bustle of the high priest's cold, night-covered courtyard. Putting ourselves in Peter's place, perhaps we can glimpse something of the passionate loyalty and guilt-ridden panic (v 26) that surge and swell around his three denials.

Sandwiching Jesus' Jewish trial between Peter's testing (Luke 22:31–34), John contrasts Jesus' openness with Peter's hiding, Jesus' truth-telling with Peter's lies. The latter's 'I am not' rebuttals (vs 17,25) stand in stark, sad relief against the two 'I am' affirmations we heard from Jesus yesterday. Not only is Peter denying his relationship with Jesus, he is also hiding something of who he is. Who he is, who we are, who we say he is, and who he says we are – these are deeply interconnected truths. Discipleship is decision and relationship, but it is also identity.

... So they asked him, 'You aren't one of his disciples, too, are you?' He denied it, saying, 'I am not.'

**John 18:25**

## RESPOND
Listen to 'Who You Say I Am' by Hillsong Worship,* and/or pray through its lyrics.

*https://www.youtube.com/watch?v=RiRKTvqsnlw

**Bible in a year:** Deuteronomy 23,24; Romans 5

# Traditions and truth

## PREPARE
What traditions (personal, local, family or faith) are precious to you? Why?

## READ
**John 18:28-40**

## EXPLORE
As the day of Passover preparations dawns, John's account is layered with irony. Bent on celebrating the festival and bound by ritual requirements (v 28), the chief priests press charges against their true High Priest, unknowingly participating in the sacrifice of their true Passover Lamb (John 1:29). Adhering to their Sabbath traditions, they evade religious and regional law (v 31); in avoiding defilement, they miss their Deliverer. They even demand Barabbas, a criminal, whose name means 'son of the father', in exchange for the righteous Son of the Father (v 40).

It's not just the religious leaders: Pilate dismisses truth before Truth himself (v 38; John 14:6). But most of their discussion centres on Jesus' kingdom – a reign of a different nature to any originating in the world (v 36). The charge of claiming kingship was a political tactic designed to hook Pilate – no Roman governor

wanted to let an insurrectionist slip past. But… a carpenter from Galilee, whose followers had scattered? Did Pilate consider this a serious possibility?

Amid the clash and clamour of these regimes, Jesus focuses on and expands our understanding of his person and purposes. Truth invites us to listen to who he is and how he lives (vs 36,37).

'… the reason I was born and came into the world is to testify to the truth. Everyone on the side of truth listens to me.'
**John 18:37**

## RESPOND
Pray: 'Lord, I don't want to miss your truth when it runs counter to the world's customs and kingdoms. Teach me to listen for you in even the most unlikely places.'

**Bible in a year:** Deuteronomy 25,26; Romans 6

# Power and partnership

## PREPARE
Find a photo of yourself. As you look at it, ask God to show you how you reflect him.

. . . . . . . . . . . . . . . . . . . . . . . . . . . . . . . . . . . . . . . . . . . . . . . . . . . . . . . . . . . . . .

## READ
**John 19:1–16a**

## EXPLORE
Violence, mockery, attempted vindication and renewed accusations follow thick and fast in today's verses. From the soldiers' sneering (v 3) to Pilate's indignant boasts of power (v 10), the passage turns on the subject of sovereignty.

We find ourselves on the sixth day of the Jewish week, the creation day on which God made living creatures and then humankind to co-reign with him (Genesis 1:24–28). From the start, man was meant to have his Maker as king, to be his ambassador, exemplifying and exercising his rule on earth. As God's people wandered from him, a succession of anointed leaders was appointed to mediate his ways and words. But that wasn't enough: Israel rejected God's reign in favour of a human king (1 Samuel 8:7).

Now we see humankind, the creature made in his image, using its God-given authority to kill the Creator and obliterate his perfect Image. With cries of 'Crucify!' and declarations of allegiance to Caesar (v 15), the chief priests bring this biblical storyline to its darkest hour. Yet, while his people reject it and Pilate fails to recognise it, Jesus – the true Man – shows us what it looks like to fulfil God's invitation to rule with him. Life here and now is our opportunity to join him and practise for eternity (Revelation 22:5).

But they shouted, 'Take him away! ... Crucify him!' 'Shall I crucify your king?' Pilate asked. 'We have no king but Caesar,' the chief priests answered.

**John 19:15**

## RESPOND
Think of the coming day. How might you step into co-reigning with God (Revelation 22:5)?

. . . . . . . . . . . . . . . . . . . . . . . . . . . . . . . . . . . . . . . . . . . . . . . . . . . . . . . . . . . . . .

**Bible in a year:** Deuteronomy 27,28; Romans 7

# All part of the plan

## PREPARE

Are you a planner, or do you prefer to live more spontaneously? What are the pros and cons?

## READ

**John 19:16b–27**

## EXPLORE

John's account of the moment of Jesus' crucifixion is surprisingly succinct. Did it pain him to dwell on what he had seen and heard? He points us to Pilate's notice (a retaliatory snub to the Jewish leaders: vs 21,22), proclaiming loud and clear, in empire-encompassing languages, the supposed crime Jesus had committed. Intended as a deterrent, it became a declaration: this is how God's true representative, partnering with his true reign, redeems the rebels and restores the ruins of his creation.

What's remarkable about this and how the soldiers fulfil detailed scriptural prophecies (v 24), is that those acting against God unknowingly participate in his plan. I find this incredibly reassuring! Our God takes the work of wicked powers and people and turns it to good (Genesis 50:20; Romans 8:28). If he can do that, what match are my mistakes for him?! If nothing in all creation can derail his purposes or separate us from his love (Romans 8:31–39), we've nothing and no one to fear – not even ourselves.

Providing for Mary in his final moments, Jesus remains true to God's words and ways. Knowing that God's faithfulness to his good, spoken, sovereign plans is unstoppable enables us to look beyond ourselves, whatever we face. This is the solid foundation for remaining true to him and all he's made us to be.

This happened that the scripture might be fulfilled that said, 'They divided my clothes among them and cast lots for my garment.'

**John 19:24**

## RESPOND

Think about how God's words have been fulfilled in your life.

**Bible in a year:** Deuteronomy 29,30; Psalm 36

# What endings are for

## PREPARE

Take time to be quiet, becoming aware of God's presence with you. Focus on your breathing, or prayerfully repeat Jesus' name.

## READ

**John 19:28–42**

## EXPLORE

Eyewitness details and words of deep significance walk us through Jesus' death and burial. What John understands in retrospect is that Jesus was sovereign over the end of his earthly life and knew the spiritual story being written (v 28). What he understood in the moment was the truth that Jesus' fully human body was unmistakably, medically dead (v 34).

Endings, especially those unwanted or unexpected, often carry painful questions. What would the woman at the well have thought if she had heard the Living Water say, 'I am thirsty' (v 28)? What might Nicodemus, who first spoke with Jesus about rebirth, have felt as he buried that broken body (vs 38–40)? What about Lazarus, if he had seen the One who called him out of the tomb carried into the darkness (vs 41,42)? What about you?

Here, on the seventh day, 'the true' rests, and hinges into 'the new'. The place we turn, slowly, waiting and wondering, is an ending – a tomb. Full of disappointment, full of questions, full of all that is finished… empty of breath, hope and laughter. Yet beyond our knowing, these pivotal places are pregnant with power and purpose: true life is about to birth new life.

> At the place where Jesus was crucified, there was a garden, and in the garden a new tomb, in which no one had ever been laid.
>
> **John 19:41**

## RESPOND

Bring to mind an ending you are experiencing. Imagine yourself facing the truth of it. Express your feelings; ask your questions. Wait here as long as you like, allowing the picture to unfold.

**Bible in a year:** Deuteronomy 31,32; Romans 8

**Sunday 31 March**
John 20:1–10

# Seeing what's not there

## PREPARE
Search for the 'Rubin's vase' optical illusion online. What do you see first – the vase or the faces?

## READ
**John 20:1–10**

## EXPLORE

'It's been moved!' Arriving in the still dark hours of the early morning (v 1), Mary found the stone rolled away. Someone else had got there sooner. Surely it had to be graverobbers? Running, breathless conversation, more running, and Peter tumbles into the tomb, with John more tentatively behind. There, the linen cloths tell a different story. No one taking the body – friend or foe – would have had the time or inclination to remove the graveclothes, never mind folding them neatly (vs 6,7). Realising that Jesus' body no longer rests there and hasn't been robbed, John's heart stirs (v 8). Belief settles more deeply, sending out new roots and shoots that will soon be nurtured into understanding by scripture and Spirit (v 9).

Seeing, believing... and later, understanding. Is that the way we'd like it to go? Certainly, there's a grace in seeing (whether in person, as the apostles did, or through scripture and other sources as we do now) coming first. But would we prefer understanding to precede believing – especially when we encounter unexpected emptiness or inexplicable events? What we see and believe in God's apparent absence is significant. Even in our breathless confusion, the shrouds of mystery we find can point us to the truth of who he is and the new life he gives.

> Finally the other disciple, who had reached the tomb first, also went inside. He saw and believed.
>
> **John 20:8**

## RESPOND
Pray: 'Lord Jesus, I want to see, believe and understand more of you and the new life you invite me into. Open my eyes. Enable my belief. Enrich my understanding.'

**Bible in a year:** Deuteronomy 33,34; Romans 9